PROBLEM SOLVING 101

PROBLEM SOLVING 101

A SIMPLE BOOK FOR SMART PEOPLE

KEN WATANABE

PORTFOLIO

PORTFOLIO

Published by the Penguin Group

Penguin Group (USA) Inc., 375 Hudson Street, New York, New York 10014, U.S.A. • Penguin Group (Canada), 90 Eglinton Avenue East, Suite 700, Toronto, Ontario, Canada M4P 2Y3 (a division of Pearson Penguin Canada Inc.) • Penguin Books Ltd, 80 Strand, London WC2R 0RL, England • Penguin Ireland, 25 St. Stephen's Green, Dublin 2, Ireland (a division of Penguin Books Ltd) • Penguin Books Australia Ltd, 250 Camberwell Road, Camberwell, Victoria 3124, Australia (a division of Pearson Australia Group Pty Ltd) • Penguin Books India Pvt Ltd, 11 Community Centre, Panchsheel Park, New Delhi – 110 017, India • Penguin Group (NZ), 67 Apollo Drive, Rosedale, North Shore 0632, New Zealand (a division of Pearson New Zealand Ltd) • Penguin Books (South Africa) (Pty) Ltd, 24 Sturdee Avenue, Rosebank, Johannesburg 2196, South Africa

Penguin Books Ltd, Registered Offices:
80 Strand, London WC2R 0RL, England

First published in 2009 by Portfolio,
a member of Penguin Group (USA) Inc.

10 9 8 7 6 5 4 3 2 1

Originally published in Japanese by Diamond Inc., Osaka.

Illustrations by Allan Sanders

LIBRARY OF CONGRESS CATALOGING IN PUBLICATION DATA
Watanabe, Ken.
Problem solving 101 : a simple book for smart people / Ken Watanabe.
    p. cm.
ISBN 978-1-59184-242-2
1. Problem solving. I. Title. II. Title: Problem solving one hundred one.
BF449.W37 2009
153.4'3—dc22   2008042023

Printed in the United States of America
Set in Chaparral Pro with Gotham and Providence
Designed by Daniel Lagin

what is your delta?

CONTENTS

Preface ix

CLASS #1:
Problem-Solving Kid Basics 1

CLASS #2:
Rock Bands and Root Causes 23

CLASS #3:
Fishy Goals and Solid Achievements 57

CLASS #4:
Soccer School Pros and Cons 85

Acknowledgments 111

PROBLEM-SOLVING TOOL BOXES:

Logic Tree 17

Yes/No Tree 32

Problem-Solving Design Plan 39

Hypothesis Pyramid 70

Pros and Cons; Criteria and Evaluation 92

PREFACE

WHY PROBLEM SOLVING?

We all have to make decisions. Whether you're a student, a parent, a businessperson, or the president of the United States, you face problems every day that need solving. The problems may vary. Maybe you need to pass a math class, or decide where to live, or figure out how to improve your company's bottom line. Maybe you want to lose some weight or simply get better at golf.

Whether the issue is big or small, we all set goals for ourselves, face challenges, and strive to overcome them. There's a fundamental approach to solving these real-life problems, one that can consistently lead you to effective and satisfying solutions. And chances are, no one has ever bothered to show you how.

One of my missions in writing this book was to show everyone a simple way to deal with the problems they face in their everyday lives. But I wasn't just trying to communicate a skill set. Being a problem solver isn't just an ability; it's a whole mind-set, one that drives people to bring out the best in themselves and to shape the world in a positive way. Rather than accepting the status quo, true problem solvers are constantly trying to proactively shape their environment. Imagine how different our world would be if leaders like Mahatma Gandhi, Martin Luther King Jr., Eleanor Roosevelt, JFK, and Steve Jobs lacked this attitude.

I hope this book will help inspire both children and adults to develop this proactive mind-set by first tackling the problems in their own lives. Once you learn this simple way to solve the personal challenges you face every day, you just might see that your bigger dreams and accomplishments are also within your reach.

WHY I WROTE THIS BOOK

Before I wrote this book, I was a consultant for the global management consulting firm of McKinsey & Company. For six years I worked with major companies all over the world to help solve their business challenges using a straightforward yet powerful set of problem-solving tools.

These are tools that anyone can use. They don't require complicated computer software or a room full of expert analysts. They're simply approaches to broaden and organize one's thinking about a problem, so that more possible solutions become clear.

In 2007 Japan's prime minister made education his nation's top agenda. As the country turned its focus to the educational system, I felt compelled to do my part. Although Japanese business leaders, educators, and politicians have long talked about the need for Japan to shift from "memorization-focused education" to "problem-solving-focused education," no one had figured out a concrete and effective way to make this happen.

So I left McKinsey to write this book and to teach kids. My aim was to teach Japanese children how to think like problem solvers, to take a proactive role in their own education and in shaping their lives. I tried to frame the tools we used at McKinsey in a fun and approachable way, one that would show kids what a practical approach to problem solving could help them accomplish. Although I don't claim to be any kind of expert on education, I hoped that the book would at least provide a starting point, one that would help shift the debate from whether we should teach problem solving to how we should go about teaching it.

Then a surprising thing happened: The book took off—and not just with kids. It first caught fire in the business segment, becoming Japan's number one business best-seller in 2007. Then it spread through the education community and to a wider general audience. It turned out that adult readers in Japan, from parents and teachers to CEOs of major corporations, had been craving a simple and useful guide to problem-solving techniques.

Now I'm focusing on helping kids put *Problem Solving 101* into practice. I think the experience kids get from having an idea, taking initiative, and learning from both their successes and their failures is what we have to put more emphasis on. So I'm creating more opportunities for them to learn more from real-life situations rather than just in the classroom.

When I work with kids, I don't start by teaching the skills from *Problem Solving 101* in a classroom. Instead, I let them learn the same way Warren Buffett did. Buffett got his first business experience when he was only six years old, buying Coke bottles from his grandfather's store and selling them for a profit. The kids I work with get to run a food and drink business using a 1965 VW van I've renovated for use as a transportable shop. The kids decide what food and drinks to sell, where to sell, and how to compete against other teams by actually selling what they have cooked or prepared. The kids learn the importance of not just problem solving skills, but also leadership, teamwork, creativity, persistence, charm, and *kaizen* (continuous improvement) to make their vision come true. Only after this experience do I help them ask the important questions and provide them with the problem-solving tools that could help them with future projects.

The value of problem-solving-oriented thinking obviously extends far beyond the classroom into every facet of our lives. It enables us to take control of the challenges we encounter and to change the world in a positive way. My hope is that English-reading audiences will benefit from the book in the same way many Japanese readers have.

Best,
Ken Watanabe

PROBLEM SOLVING 101

CLASS #1

PROBLEM-SOLVING KID BASICS

YOU'RE NEVER TOO OLD TO BECOME A PROBLEM-SOLVING KID

This is a book about kids solving problems. They face some pretty tricky challenges—the kinds of problems that might cause most people to throw up their hands and give up. But problem-solving kids aren't like most people—even though most people should be more like them.

As you'll see, problem-solving kids come in all ages, shapes, and sizes. They may seem to have special talents, or at least more than their fair share of luck. But the truth is, they're people just like you, who have learned how to think, make decisions and act on their own, and to live proactive lives. They've also picked up some helpful problem-solving tools along the way.

If you follow the simple lessons in these pages, you too can become a problem-solving kid (even if you consider yourself a grown-up). Rather than feeling as though your life is out of your control, you can take charge and shape the world around you. Instead of being overwhelmed by the challenges you face every day, you can learn to enjoy them and overcome them.

In fact, you may even feel like a better person at the end of this course. Your dreams and goals will seem less out of reach. And you'll be better able to accomplish whatever you're passionate enough and imaginative enough to conceive and pursue.

It could be something as simple as becoming a better dancer or learning how to cook French cuisine. Or maybe it's a bigger goal, like running for president or solving the global warming crisis. Whatever it is, you'll learn how to tackle it.

Problem solving isn't a talent limited to the lucky few. It's actually a skill and a habit that you can learn. This book will introduce you to a basic problem-solving approach through three case studies:

- The Mushroom Lovers, a new band trying to improve their concert attendance numbers
- John Octopus, a bright young man with aspirations of becoming a computer graphics animator who needs to buy his first computer
- Kiwi, an aspiring soccer player looking for the best training school in Brazil

It will also give you a full toolbox of proven problem-solving techniques, the same techniques used by successful problem-solving people and companies all over the world. But before we start learning the problem-solving approach, let me introduce you to the problem-solving kids and their friends.

PROBLEM-SOLVING KIDS AND COMPANY

So by now you're probably wondering what is it exactly that makes someone a problem-solving kid. First, let's talk about what they're not. There are several common attitudes that can get in the way of effective problem solving. While the following characters may sound like caricatures of real people, I bet these non-problem-solving kids also sound pretty familiar. Chances are you know people just like them at school or at work. Maybe they're your friends or members of your family. Some of them may even remind you of yourself!

For instance, take Miss Sigh.

Miss Sigh is the kind of person who gives up immediately whenever she faces even the smallest challenge. She just sighs and says, "I'll never be able to do that." Which isn't to say she *couldn't* achieve things if she tried. Sometimes she has a great idea or notices a problem that can be fixed. But she's terrified of failing and having people laugh at her. Instead of speaking up or taking action, she sits around feeling sorry for herself.

Miss Sigh can't take control of her own life. She feels as though no one understands her, and she blames anything bad that happens on everybody else. Over and over, she says the same kinds of things:

- "I'll never be able to do that. I'm just not that talented."
- "I'm not going to try. What if I fail? Everyone will make fun of me!"
- "I blame my parents. I blame society. I blame you!"

- "Nobody understands me. Nobody cares about me. Everybody is out to get me."

Mr. Critic, on the other hand, is never afraid to speak up. He is a professional criticizer. Whatever the plan, he is ready to point out the shortcomings and shoot down everyone else's ideas. If someone tries something and fails, he'll be the first to say, "I told you so." He's always eager to blame someone else whenever things go wrong.

He may have a lot to say about other people's mistakes, but he never does much of anything himself. As you probably know, being a critic is easy; getting stuff done is the real challenge. Even if you know how things should be done, it's useless if you aren't willing to roll up your sleeves and get to work. It's possible that Mr. Critic may not realize how little his criticisms are appreciated by people who are actually trying to get things accomplished. Or maybe he's too afraid to take responsibility and face the fact that he himself makes mistakes.

You may hear Mr. Critic saying things like:

- "Well, that definitely won't work. What a stupid idea!"
- "I told you that would get screwed up. It's all your fault."
- "Come on, I told you what you needed to do. Why can't you get it done?"

Mr. Critic may be a big downer, but Miss Dreamer has her head stuck in the clouds. She loves coming up with new ideas. But it rarely goes beyond that. She never bothers to figure out how to turn her ideas into real plans, and she definitely doesn't try to get anything done. She is satisfied just thinking about her great dreams. They're always better in her head than they would be in reality, anyway.

Miss Dreamer has many audacious dreams—dreams that never seem to become realities:

- "I want to write a novel!"
- "Wouldn't it be great if I started my own business?"
- "I want to be a doctor when I grow up."
- "I'm an idea person. Don't bother me with the nitty gritty details!"

Mr. Go-Getter may not seem like a non–problem solver when you first meet him. He's definitely not one to worry about problems or entertain negative thoughts. And when something goes wrong, he quickly jumps into action. His attitude is "I can't change the past. But I can do something now." Mr. Go-Getter's tenacity and proactiveness are definitely positive traits.

However, if he knew how to pause and think for a minute before rushing to execute, he would be able to achieve so much more. He also tends to blame every failure on a simple lack of effort—he thinks any problem can be solved by trying harder. When he makes up his mind about how to solve a problem, he refuses to change course. He's not interested in seeking out the root cause of his problems or in considering alternative solutions. He just doesn't realize that stopping to think can be just as important as taking action.

Mr. Go-Getter can often be heard saying things like:

- "I'll never give up. I've got to overcome this challenge!"
- "I've got to try harder! I can't stop now!"
- "I know this will work if I just put in a little more effort."
- "Why stop to think? That's just a waste of time. Everything is about execution!"

Are you one of these types? Do you ever find yourself sighing and giving up? Do you think it's easier to criticize other people rather than trying to do anything on your own? Do you love to dream but hate to plan? Do you attack problems head on but fail to turn on the brakes when you aren't getting anything done? Or are you more like a problem-solving kid?

Problem-solving kids have a real flair for setting goals and getting things accomplished. They take overcoming challenges in stride. Like Mr. Go-Getter, they don't agonize over problems. However, unlike Mr. Go-Getter, they think about the root causes of their problems and map out an effective plan before and while taking action, and they are willing to rework their plan as new challenges pop up. By striking a balance between thinking and acting, they can accomplish amazing things. Problem-solving kids enjoy learning from their successes as well as from their failures.

The tool kit of a problem-solving kid includes identifying the root cause of a problem and setting specific goals. They have positive attitudes and stay focused on what can be changed rather than what already happened. They come up with specific action plans to fix their problems and then execute right away. Once they take action, they constantly monitor their own progress.

Here's what you may hear from a problem-solving kid:

- "Okay! I'm going to accomplish this within three months."
- "This is a problem, but rather than worrying about it, I'm going to figure out what I can do about it."
- "So what really caused this?"
- "To fix this, we're going to need to do X, Y, and Z. Let's try them out."
- "So how did this work out? What went wrong? Is there a way we could do this better next time?"

Take a look at the following chart. It compares the five characters we've just met and highlights their differences.

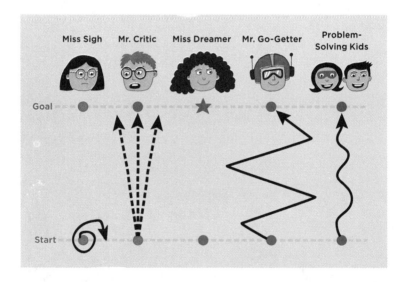

In the chart, all five characters have a problem they need to solve.

Miss Sigh circles around the starting point, sighing away. Of course, she gets nowhere.

Mr. Critic is certain he knows how the problem should be solved, and he quickly points out to others what they are doing wrong. But he doesn't do anything, and his criticisms don't help anyone else get the problem solved, either. The dotted lines from his starting point are all the other people's plans that he shot down.

Miss Dreamer does not get to the goal, either. She just stares at the goal like it's a bright, beautiful star. Sitting at the starting point, she dreams of grand and wonderful solutions to the problem, but never tries to make them happen.

Unlike the first three, Mr. Go-Getter at least tries to reach the goal. He never gives up and just keeps on running as fast and as hard as he can. However, he is not necessarily running in the right direction. When he figures out that he's going the wrong way, he turns and starts running in another wrong direction as fast as he can. He never stops to identify the root cause of his problem or figure out an effective plan. It's a shame, because he certainly has more than enough motivation to reach his goal.

The problem-solving kids achieve their goal more quickly and directly than the others. While they have plenty of Mr. Go-Getter's guts and speedy execution, they also figure out the actual root cause of the problem they need to solve before coming up with an actionable plan and going to work. As they travel toward their goal, they never stop monitoring their own progress to make sure they're headed in the right direction. While others get nowhere or head in

the wrong direction, the problem-solving kids have already reached that first goal and are heading for the next one.

Problem solving isn't a talent that some people have and others don't. It's a habit. By developing the right skills and adopting the right attitude, anyone can become a problem-solving kid.

Problem-Solving Kids Evolve at an Amazing Rate

Problem-solving kids don't just reach their goals faster; they evolve faster, too. They check out the impact of their actions and try to learn from their successes as well as their failures.

If you never take action, you'll never get any feedback on your attempts, and without feedback, you'll never grow as a problem-solving kid. That great idea in your head will remain just that—only an idea. When you do take action, every result is an opportunity to reflect and learn valuable lessons. Even if what you take away from your assessment seems to be of small consequence, all of these small improvements taken together make a huge difference in the long term.

Let's look at an example: Alex, Bianca, and Cliff all own fruit stands that each sells 100 watermelons per month. Alex's business increases at a rate of 1 percent each month, while Bianca's increases by 5 percent, and Cliff's increases by 10 percent. How different would their watermelon sales be in three years?

After three years, Alex will be selling 143 watermelons a month. However, Bianca will be selling 579 watermelons, while Cliff will be selling a whopping 3,091 watermelons every month. While Bianca is selling more than five times as many watermelons as Alex, Cliff is selling twenty-two times more than Alex. He is going to need a bigger fruit stand for all those watermelons. Imagine what the difference would be over a longer time period, like ten years, or thirty!

In the following chart, Cliff's business growth soars above his more slowly improving competitors. That seemingly small 10 percent rate of improvement means a lot in the long run.

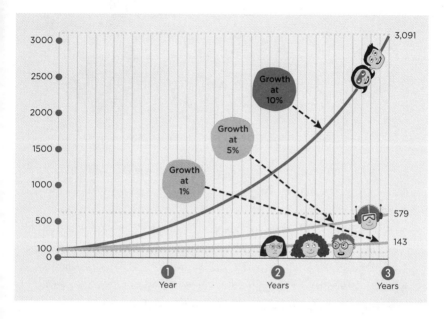

Through both your successful and unsuccessful experiences, your problem-solving skills can develop beyond solving your own problems to actually shaping your environment. You may start by leading your sports team or school or community to do greater things. Maybe you'll even create a great business or solve some of the world's most challenging problems.

WHAT IS PROBLEM SOLVING?

Problem solving is a process that can be broken down into four steps: (1) understand the current situation; (2) identify the root cause of the problem; (3) develop an effective action plan; and (4) execute until the problem is solved, making modifications as necessary.

These steps come as a package. Before you can solve anything, you first need to realize that there's a problem. Once you do, identifying the root cause of the problem isn't enough. You have to think through how you could fix the problem, and then actually

13

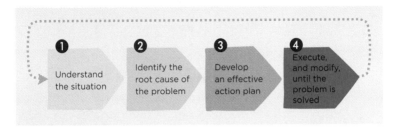

take the actions required to fix it. Problem solving is a combination of thinking and acting. Just doing one or the other won't get you anywhere.

You might think this sounds really simple. The catch is that we often don't do what seems simple and obvious. For example, consider a student whose math grades are going down. Like many people, he might just say, "I have to raise my grades," and hope for the best without actually doing anything to improve them. Chances are that his math grades are going to stay right where they are, because he never bothers to figure out the root cause of his problem and what he can do about it.

Or maybe the student decides, "I have to quit the soccer team so I have more time to study." Even with this drastic action, his grades may not improve if it turns out the real problem was not how long he studies, but how effectively he studies. Why give up the chance to play soccer with your friends for nothing?

So what would a problem-solving kid do in this situation? Let's look at an example:

A problem-solving kid may start by asking himself, "What types of questions am I getting wrong?" Then he could break the questions into categories, like algebra, fractions, and geometry. By comparing his scores by category, he may find that his algebra score is actually going up, while his score in fractions is flat, and really only his geometry scores are going down. Just looking at the average trend of the math grades as a whole doesn't help him see what is really happening.

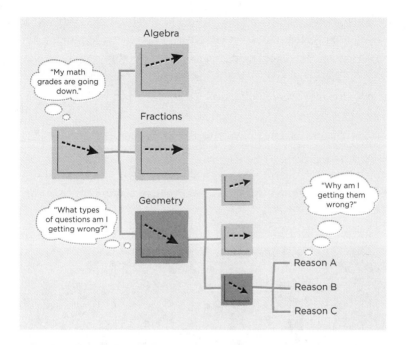

So if geometry seems to be the only area causing the grade to drop, the next step would be to further break down the geometry scores into additional subtopics, including area, angles, and volume, to better identify what types of problems are causing him trouble.

When his understanding of the situation goes from the level of "My math grades are going down" to the much more nuanced "My math grades are going down because I am not doing well in three topics: trapezoid area, cylinder volume, and Pythagorean theorem application," the effectiveness of his plan and the end result will be significantly different.

Once the problem-solving kid has identified what types of problems he is getting wrong, his next step is to figure out exactly what he should do to perform better. Should he increase the time he spends studying math, improve his productivity when he does study, or both? To increase his math study time, he could decide to wake up thirty minutes earlier or take thirty minutes before going to sleep to practice solving these types of problems. Improving his productivity means changing his approach to studying. He could switch to a better textbook, ask his teacher or friends to help him go over his most challenging problems after school, or ask his parents to hire a tutor.

The reason math grades go down are different for everybody. So, naturally, the most effective way to solve a math-skills problem would also be different for everybody. This is why you have to keep asking the "why" and the "how" to develop a custom-made action plan.

As you can see, problem solving is not complicated. All you have to do is understand the situation, identify the root cause, develop an effective plan, and execute. Even if the problem you face is big and complicated, if you learn how to break it down into smaller, manageable problems, you will be able to solve it.

Once you learn the basic problem-solving approach, you can stop panicking and gain the confidence to solve any problems that you face in life, whether they are about grades, work, or your personal life.

PROBLEM-SOLVING TOOL BOX:
LOGIC TREE

A logic tree is a great tool to use when you problem solve. It's a visual tool that helps when you are trying to identify all the potential root causes of a problem and generate a wide variety of solutions.

The key to making a useful logic tree is to break down a problem into categories without leaving anything out, and to group similar items under the same branch.

This will make more sense if we start with an easy example. How would you break down a class of third-graders? One way is to break it down by gender: boys and girls. Another way is to break it down by height: taller than four feet, four feet or shorter. You could also break it down by the dominant hand: right-handed, left-handed, or both.

The logic trees for these breakdowns would look like this:

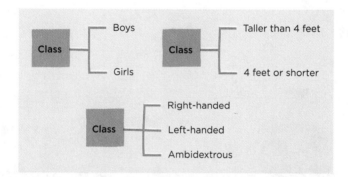

Pretty simple, right? Did you notice that that when you create the branches, no one gets left out and none of the branches overlap one another?

Now, how would you break down a class according to the clubs students belong to?

Were you able to create a logic tree that is not missing anything and that does not overlap?

When you create the logic tree, you don't necessarily have to build it from left to right. Simply start by listing whatever comes to mind on a piece of paper. To build the tree, group major topics (e.g., "Belongs to a school club") on the left, moving to more minor or limited topics (e.g., "Sports," "Art," etc.) to the right. Group similar topics together ("Team sports," "Mainly individual sports"). The next step is to create more branches.

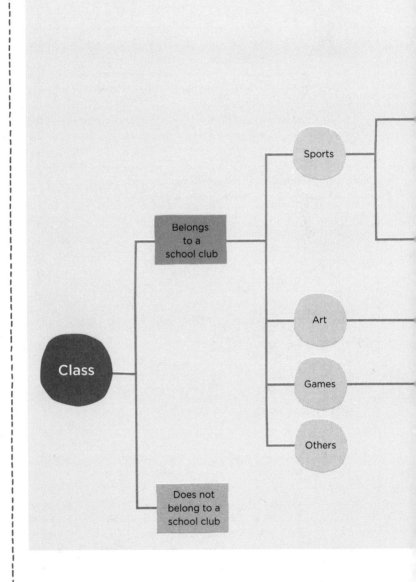

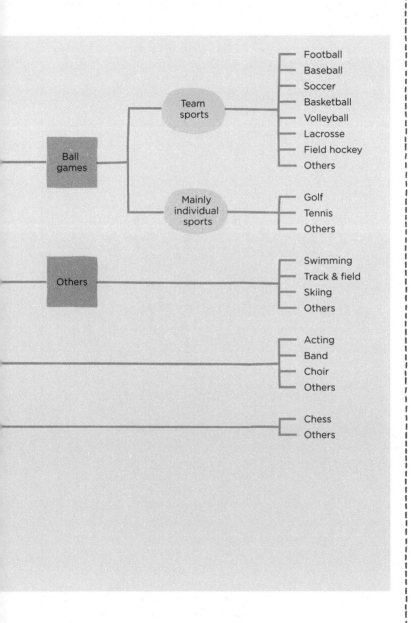

Starting at the right, for each group of topics, ask yourself, "What can I call this group to sum it up?" Draw a branch to the left and write the name of that group. From the left side of the tree, for each bigger topic ask, "Specifically what or how?" to add sub-branches out to the right. Just like the logic tree above, the finished tree grows bigger from left to right.

Let's try one more example:

How do you increase the amount of pepper that comes out of a pepper shaker without changing the strength or speed you use to shake the bottle? Use a logic tree to come up with as many ideas as possible. (And let's assume humidity is not an issue.)

How did it go? Here is one potential solution:

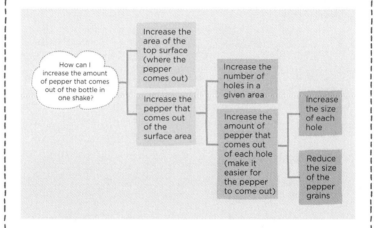

To build this tree, you start with the problem on the left: "How can I increase the amount of pepper that comes out of the bottle in one shake?" You can then begin building branches by coming up with possible solutions. Two possible solutions are (1) to increase the area of the top surface, or (2) to increase the amount of pepper that comes out of the surface area. To branch out from the second option, two possible ways to increase the amount of pepper from the surface area are (1) to increase the number of holes in a given area, or (2) to increase the amount of pepper that comes out of each hole. Finally, you can increase the amount of pepper that comes out of each hole by increasing the size of each hole or by reducing the size of the pepper grains. In fact, increasing the size of the holes is how one major spice company increased its sales!

Sometimes when you're developing a logic tree it helps to draw a picture. It will help you identify the parameters that can be changed.

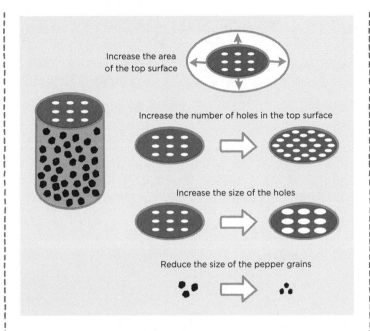

Increase the area of the top surface

Increase the number of holes in the top surface

Increase the size of the holes

Reduce the size of the pepper grains

It may take you a while to get the knack for making logic trees, but once you master it, it will help you to think beyond the initial spark of an idea and lead you to come up with new and effective solutions to your problems.

In the following classes, we'll see how the problem-solving approach and tools are used by various problem-solving kids: a rock band called the Mushroom Lovers, who want to increase their concert attendance; John Octopus, who wants to buy a computer as a first step toward achieving his dream of becoming an animator and a Hollywood movie director working with computer-generated imagery (CGI); and Kiwi, an aspiring soccer player trying to find the best school in Brazil to hone her skills.

CLASS #2

ROCK BANDS AND ROOT CAUSES

L ife is full of challenges. We all face obstacles as we try to accomplish our goals and dreams. Even the problems that pop up in our daily lives can be overwhelming.

But that doesn't mean you should just give up!

Instead, try stepping back and figuring out the root cause of the problems and how you can overcome them.

The process is very similar to how doctors treat their patients. Think about what doctors do when you visit them when you're not well: They first ask you some questions about your symptoms and then take your temperature. They may also run blood tests or take X-rays. They are collecting information and analyzing it to identify the root cause of your illness. Only after they've determined the diagnosis do they decide what to prescribe, whether it's medicine for a cold or surgery to remove a tumor. Remember the difference between the symptom (headache), the root cause (fever), and the prescription (take cold medicine). The better you get at understanding the symptoms and identifying the root causes, the better you will get at developing effective solutions.

In this chapter, we'll follow a very similar process. Here's the approach:

- Step 1: Diagnose the situation and identify the root cause of the problem.

    1A List all the potential root causes of the problem.
    1B Develop a hypothesis for the likely root cause.
    1C Determine the analyses and information required to test the hypothesis.
    1D Analyze and identify the root cause.

- Step 2: Develop the solution.

    2A Develop a wide variety of solutions to solve the problem.
    2B Prioritize actions.
    2C Develop an implementation plan.

Let's see how this process works through a case study: a struggling young rock band called the Mushroom Lovers.

MISS MUSHROOM

EGGPLANT

TOFU

SAVE THE MUSHROOM LOVERS!

Three years ago, Miss Mushroom and two of her friends, Eggplant and Tofu, formed a rock band called the Mushroom Lovers.

It all started when Miss Mushroom went to see the Rolling Stones at Madison Square Garden. Right after the concert, Miss Mushroom called up Eggplant and Tofu, bursting with excitement. "Hey, we are going to start a rock band tomorrow," she told them. "Of course, I am the singer. Eggplant, you play the guitar! Tofu, you're going to be the drummer, all right? We'll meet up right after school tomorrow and start practicing!"

"Wait a second—" Eggplant said.

"Hold on there—" Tofu said.

But Miss Mushroom hung up the phone as soon as she was done doling out her instructions. Eggplant and Tofu gave a deep sigh. "Here we go again," they said. But they both love Miss Mushroom, and whenever she really wants something, they try to do whatever it takes to make her dream come true.

That day, Eggplant borrowed his big brother's guitar and started teaching himself how to play. Tofu practiced playing the drums by using a pair of chopsticks and a cardboard box until he was able to buy a used drum a year later after saving some money. Miss Mushroom's singing was so horrible that Eggplant and Tofu had to wear earplugs to block out her noise. But over the past three years she has improved dramatically and now has a great husky voice. "We aren't bad, eh?" Miss Mushroom said with a big smile after every rehearsal.

Three months ago, Eggplant, Tofu, and Miss Mushroom were walking home from school. Eggplant and Tofu were trying to tell Miss Mushroom about their math test that afternoon, but she didn't seem to be listening. She just kept responding, "Yup, yup" with her little nod. Her mind seemed to be somewhere else. Suddenly, she stopped walking and announced, "We are going to put on a concert at the high school gymnasium next Saturday! We're going to do it every month now. All right?!"

"Next Saturday!? That's impossible!" said Eggplant.

"The school won't let us use the gymnasium. Students never rent the gymnasium for their personal use!" Tofu exclaimed.

Miss Mushroom steamed up like a kettle. She hates hearing things like "That is impossible" or "Nobody has ever done that."

"What is wrong with you guys!" she yelled. "I hate those words! We are trying to become a professional band, right? How are we going to start playing in front of big crowds if we don't start soon? I am going to go see the principal right now and ask him to allow us to use the gymnasium. Eggplant and Tofu, you guys start letting people know about our concert. Now get to work!"

Miss Mushroom turned around and ran back toward the school. Eggplant and Tofu looked at each other and sighed, "What do we do now?"

Miss Mushroom is great at getting things done and doesn't hesitate to use her charm when necessary. She got permission from the principal to use the gymnasium right away. Eggplant and Tofu told a few of their friends about the concert, and the event was held as planned.

Three months passed and the Mushroom Lovers had put on three concerts. But Miss Mushroom seemed very angry again. "Why are there only fifteen people in the crowd when I am spending my precious time to put on a show!? We had only ten people at the first concert and fifteen at the second, and fifteen again at the third. What is the problem? Weren't you guys responsible for packing the gymnasium with people? It's already the fourth concert! Make sure the place is full this time!"

Seeing Miss Mushroom's teary eyes, Eggplant and Tofu swore to themselves to find out the root cause of their attendance problem and fill up the gymnasium for the next concert.

Diagnose the Situation and Identify the Root Cause

1A. LIST ALL THE POTENTIAL ROOT CAUSES OF THE PROBLEM

Very few people are coming to the Mushroom Lovers' concerts. The band wants to find out why and what they can do about it.

Let's start with the why: Why are people not coming to the concerts? What could be the reason?

It turns out that there are many potential reasons, not just one.

For people to attend the concert, they must first be aware that the concert exists. Then they must want to come to the concert, and hopefully they'll want to continue to come to other concerts after seeing the Mushroom Lovers' amazing show.

Therefore, as you can see in the following logic tree, some people may not have been aware of the concert in the first place (A); others may have been aware of the concert but either did not want to go or had another reason they could not attend (B); and others may have gone once but did not continue going to future shows (C).

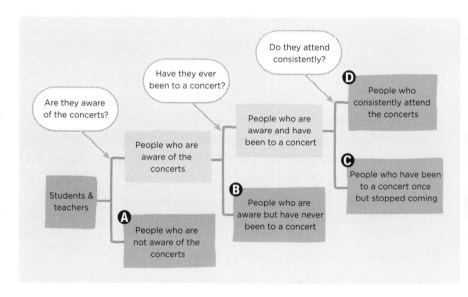

This logic tree can also be transformed into a yes/no tree. A yes/no tree groups people or objects into buckets based on the answers to yes/no questions. By assigning everyone and everything involved to a bucket, you can more clearly see what the core issue is. For the logic tree above, the related yes/no tree creates buckets using the following questions:

❶ Are they aware of the concerts?

❷ If they are aware, have they ever been to a concert?

❸ If they have been to a concert, do they attend consistently?

Everybody *must* fall into one of the buckets without exception.

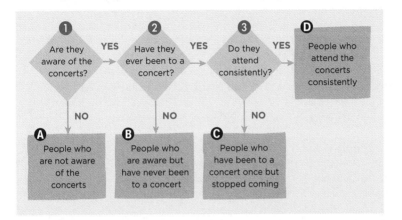

To identify the root cause of their attendance problem, Eggplant and Tofu need to find out the size of each bucket. Then they need to further consider the questions:

- "Why are some people not aware of the concerts?"
- "Why don't some people come to the concerts even if they are aware of them?"
- "Why do some people stop coming to the concerts?"

PROBLEM-SOLVING TOOL BOX: YES/NO TREE

You can use a yes/no tree to help you figure out a problem's root cause or decide how to solve a problem. To create one, you answer multiple yes/no questions, like the ones Tofu and Eggplant ask in their survey.

Let's walk through another example. Imagine you've overslept. You were supposed to be up by 6 a.m. to take a shower, eat breakfast, and catch the 7:08 a.m. bus. Instead, you jump out of bed at 6:53. As you attempt to brush your teeth while pulling on your jeans, you think, "Why didn't I wake up? Did my alarm go off? Is the alarm broken?"

Assuming you aren't rushing to catch a bus right now, try to create a yes/no tree that will help you figure out why you weren't able to wake up. Write down a question, then consider whether a yes or no answer will lead to an explanation (a bucket) or another question. Repeat this process for each further question until you've created buckets for all the possible explanations.

How did it go? Here's one possible yes/no tree for why you weren't able to wake up. Your tree doesn't have to look exactly like the one shown here, but it should have used yes/no questions to help you discover all the potential causes for oversleeping.

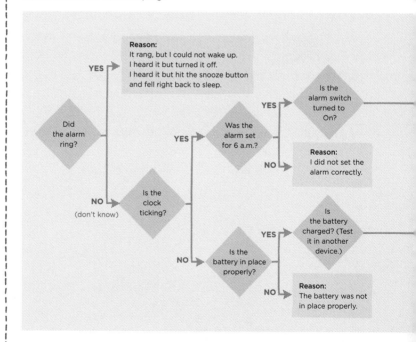

1B. DEVELOP A HYPOTHESIS FOR THE LIKELY ROOT CAUSE

Now let's come up with a hypothesis that explains why people aren't attending the concerts.

A hypothesis is a hunch. It's what you think is the most likely explanation for your problem, but you haven't yet confirmed it.

By determining your hypothesis and thinking through the reasoning that underlies it, you will be able to check whether it's right. From there, you can move on to making a sound decision that will lead to a productive solution.

Let's take an everyday example: Say one day you decide to visit your grandma who lives in a town thirty miles away. However, you realize it's the day after Thanksgiving, and every store in town is having a big sale. People will be rushing to the mall, which means traffic will be horrible. You want to spend as much quality time

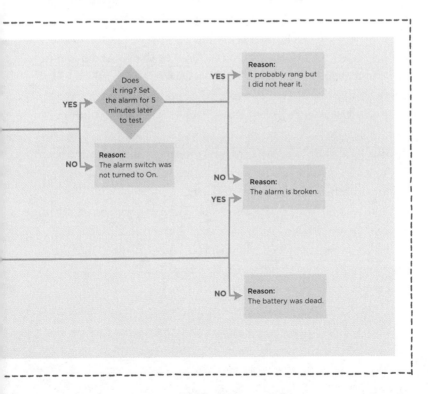

with your grandma as possible, but you need to be home by 10 p.m. because you have an early baseball practice the next day.

What happens if you just jump into action without thinking first? You always visit grandma by bus, so today is no exception. You buy a ticket, get a seat, and end up spending two hours on the bus stuck in traffic. By the time you get to grandma's house, you barely have time to kiss her on the cheek before hopping back on the bus again for the grueling trip home.

If you had stopped to think before taking the bus, the trip might have worked out differently. By making a hypothesis about the potential traffic and finding an easy way to check its validity, you would have been able to find the best travel solution and could have spent more time with your grandmother.

Your hypothesis could have been, "I should take the train instead of the bus because the traffic will be bad." The rationale for this hypothesis could then be, "The traffic must be bad because the day-after-Thanksgiving sales are going on." Fortunately, in this situation there is a quick and effective way to check your hypothesis. All you have to do is to turn on the radio or the TV and listen to the traffic report. You could also call your friend who said she was going to take the bus to see a football game and ask her about the traffic on the way there. Once you have that additional information, you could make your final decision.

This procedure is something you probably would do naturally without giving it too much thought, right? You're already a successful hypothesizer. That's all there is to it.

Now let's get back to the Mushroom Lovers. Eggplant and Tofu have come up with a hypothesis for their attendance problem: The root cause is awareness. People are not attending because they don't even know about the concerts in the first place.

Let's examine their rationale:

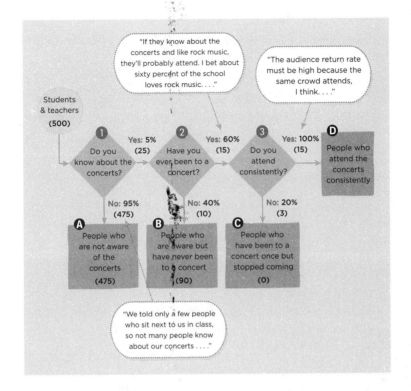

They think awareness must be low because they didn't try very hard to get the word out. As Tofu says, "We told only a few of the kids who sit next to us in class, and Miss Mushroom probably didn't invite anybody because even though she's bossy she's actually really shy." Their hypothesis is that only about one in twenty people at their school (about 5 percent) even know about the concert.

Next, they estimate that 60 percent of the people who find out about the concert would probably show up. Their rationale for this estimate is based on their guess that about 60 percent of the people at their school actually like rock music, and, according to Eggplant, "If you like rock music and find out there's a concert at your school, you'd definitely come. I would!"

Finally, they assume that the audience return rate of the people who keep coming to the concerts after seeing a show is 100 percent.

They try to remember who was in the crowd at the last three concerts. The gymnasium was pretty dark, and they were busy rocking out, so they aren't exactly sure who was there. "I think everyone in the crowd was about the same every time," Tofu says. "Since we're pretty good, once they hear us play, how could they not keep coming? Let's say one hundred percent of the people are continuing to come."

By this reasoning, they conclude that their biggest issue is awareness. If this hypothesis is true, they should focus on figuring out a way to raise awareness. So let's see if they're right.

1C. DETERMINE THE ANALYSES AND INFORMATION REQUIRED TO TEST HYPOTHESIS

Now Eggplant and Tofu need to test their hypothesis. To do this, they need to do some research.

This is where the information collection and analysis part of the problem-solving process comes into play. You're not collecting information just for the sake of collecting it, or analyzing it just for fun. You're doing it to help you make better decisions.

So what kind of analyses do Eggplant and Tofu have to conduct? And what information do they need to conduct these analyses?

Analysis #1: How many people are in each "awareness" category?
Take a look at Eggplant and Tofu's hypothesis diagram again. We can group the people at the Mushroom Lovers' school into four different groups: (1) not aware of the concert; (2) aware but not attending; (3) attended at least once; and (4) attending regularly. So how do we figure out how many people fall into each of these buckets?

It would be time consuming and difficult to meet all 500 people at the school and ask them one by one which group they fall into. Even if Miss Mushroom helped and they divided up the task, if they asked one person each day, it would take nearly half a year (167 days). So, what should they do?

After a brainstorming session on how to get the information they need, Eggplant and Tofu decide to create a list of questions and ask all the teachers to conduct a survey during Monday morning homeroom. The teachers need to ask only these three questions and write down how many students raise their hands for each one (and count their own answers as well):

1. Raise your hand if you already know about the Mushroom Lovers' monthly concerts.
2. If you knew about the Mushroom Lovers' concerts, raise your hand if you've ever been to one.
3. If you have been to a Mushroom Lovers' concert, raise your hand if you are attending them regularly.

This survey is easy and efficient. It won't take more than three minutes for the teachers to ask the questions.

Analysis #2: Why do some people who know about the concerts not attend?

Next, Eggplant and Tofu have to figure out why some people are not attending the concerts even though they are aware of them. If they had time and a lot of resources, Eggplant and Tofu could conduct a big person-by-person survey of everyone in the school. But that probably isn't necessary. If they interview about five people, they should get a pretty good idea of the main reasons. They decide to ask the teachers to jot down a few names of the people who knew about the concerts but had never attended, so they can interview them later.

Analysis #3: Why are some people not attending regularly? Will people attend regularly in the future?

Interviewing about five people will give Eggplant and Tofu a pretty good idea about the answer to these questions as well. They decide to ask for input on the good and bad points of their past concerts.

They hope they'll get valuable hints on how to improve to make sure people will keep coming back to their future shows. They know it's much easier to retain loyal fans than it is to find new ones.

Remember, Eggplant and Tofu's hypothesis is that once people come to one show, they'll continue to attend, but that may not necessarily be the case. They decide to reach out to anyone who stopped coming and find out why. Hopefully, they can learn how to turn one-time attendees into future regular fans.

People often fall into the trap of collecting information and conducting analyses just for the sake of doing them. Don't forget that the point of all this research is to help you make informed decisions. Try to collect and analyze information efficiently and effectively. This will help you make better use of your limited time and resources.

PROBLEM-SOLVING TOOL BOX:
PROBLEM-SOLVING DESIGN PLAN

If you start collecting and analyzing data without first clarifying the question you are trying to answer, you're probably doing yourself more harm than good. You'll end up drowning in a flood of information and realize only later that most of that research was a waste of time.

To avoid this problem, you should develop a problem-solving design plan before you start chasing after information. In the design plan, you clarify the issues you are trying to solve, state your current hypotheses and rationale, and list the analyses, actions, and information required to prove or disprove those hypotheses. Developing this plan before you start researching will drastically increase your problem-solving productivity.

Additionally, putting your plan down on paper will not only clarify your thoughts. If you're working in a group, this plan will also help your team focus on what needs to be done and provide the jumping-off point for your group brainstorming. You will be able to focus on only what you really need to know to make a decision.

Eggplant and Tofu's problem-solving design plan looks like this:

Issue	Hypothesis	Rationale	Analysis/ Activities	Information Source
How many people are in each category?	Most people are not aware of the concert.	We told only a few students who sit next to us in class about the concert.	Category analysis: Ask teachers to conduct a survey.	Survey
Why are some people who know about the concerts not coming?	Because they don't like rock music in general.	What music lover wouldn't want to go to a free show?	Interview 5 people who knew about the concerts but didn't attend.	Interview
Will people want to keep coming to the concerts?	Once they see one concert, most people will keep coming to future shows.	Most people at the last show were repeat fans. Also, we're very confident with our level of performance, so the audience must be satisfied.	Interview 5 people who attended a concert and ask if they will continue to come. Interview a few people (if there are any) who stopped coming and find out why.	Interview

1D. ANALYZE AND IDENTIFY THE ROOT CAUSE

Analysis #1: How many people are in each "awareness" category?

The teachers agreed to conduct the survey for Eggplant and Tofu, and the data poured in. They added together all the responses and came up with the following results:

Potential concert attendees: 500 students and teachers

- Question #1: Did you already know about the Mushroom Lovers' concerts?
- Answer #1: Yes = 150 people (30%)
  No = 350 people (70%)

- Question #2: If you knew about the Mushroom Lovers' concerts, have you ever been to one?
- Answer #2: Yes = 15 people (10%)
  No = 135 people (90%)

- Question #3: If you have been to a Mushroom Lovers' concert, do you attend them regularly?
- Answer #3: Yes = 12 people (80%)
  No = 3 people (20%)

With this data, Tofu and Eggplant are able to figure out the breakdown of people into each bucket:

- **Ⓐ** People who are not aware of the concerts: 350 people (70%)
- **Ⓑ** People who are aware but have never been to a concert: 135 people (27%)
- **Ⓒ** People who have been to a concert once but stopped coming: 3 people (1%)
- **Ⓓ** People who attend the concerts consistently: 12 people (2%)

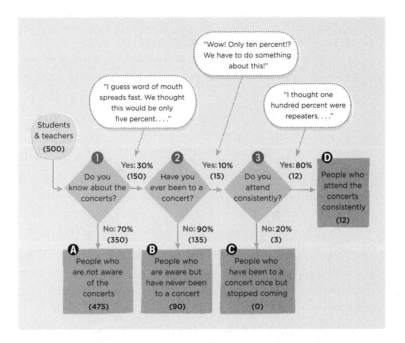

Eggplant and Tofu assumed people weren't coming to the concerts mainly because they didn't know about them, and that once everybody became aware, about 60 percent of the people would start coming (about 300 people).

But when they looked at their data, they found that 30 percent of the people were already aware of the concerts, not the 5 percent they'd assumed. It appears that the people Eggplant and Tofu invited directly and the people who came to the show talked about it and spread the word.

On the other hand, while they thought 60 percent of the people who knew about the concerts were coming, they learned the ratio was actually only 10 percent! There are many people who knew about the concerts and didn't attend. It seems that just improving the school's awareness of the concert will not drive more people to come out to watch them play. They decide that they need to find out why people are not willing to come.

However, their estimate on the percentage of people who continued to return to their concerts after attending once was not far off: That turned out to be 80 percent, compared to their initial estimate of 100 percent. But now that they know some people stopped attending, they want to find out why.

As you can see, the outcome of the analysis is often at odds with the original hypothesis. What would happen if Eggplant and Tofu had acted on their original hypothesis without checking to see if it was correct? They probably would have put up posters and distributed flyers all over the school and ended up increasing the number of spectators by a marginal amount. (Because no matter how much they raised awareness, only 10 percent of the people who knew about the show would likely come.) This is why you should test your hypothesis if you can figure out an efficient way to do so.

The following chart summarizes the difference between Eggplant and Tofu's original hypothesis and the actual results of their research.

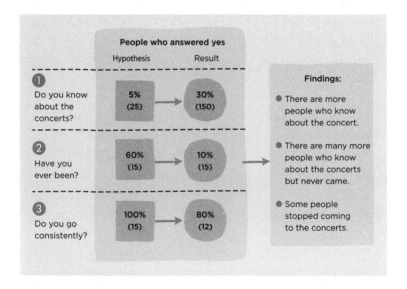

Analysis #2: Why do some people who know about the concerts not attend?

Eggplant and Tofu have found out that there are a lot of people who know about the concerts but choose not to attend. In order to figure out why, they interview five people who belong to this group.

They get a wide range of feedback:

- "Yup, I heard that you are doing a concert every month. Why don't I go? Well, I don't know what kind of music you guys play, and to be honest, I don't know how good you guys are. . . . "
- "I don't know you guys. I heard rumors about your band, but I was like, 'Who are they?'"
- "Are you kidding me? You guys are a middle school band, how can you be worth watching on a Saturday? I bet everyone thinks you guys must suck, anyway."
- "I really wanted to go, but the concert is at noon on Saturdays, right? I have baseball games then. . . . Frank and Mike couldn't go for the same reason."
- "I have no interest in music. I don't even listen to music at home. Why would I go?"

From these comments, they determine that there are three main reasons people are not attending the Mushroom Lovers' shows:

1. "They don't know what kind of music we're playing or how good we are."
2. "The show time doesn't work for their schedule."
3. "They're not interested in music in the first place."

"Interesting!" Tofu exclaims. "It may be tough to get people who are not interested in music to come, but we could definitely do something about people who are not coming because they don't know what kind of music we play or how good we are, and people whose schedules don't work." Eggplant and Tofu conduct ten additional interviews and figure out that more people would be able to come if they moved the concert to Saturday evening. "Wow," Eggplant says. "I think we can do something about this!" They're starting to feel hopeful now that they have a much better understanding of the root cause of their problem.

Analysis #3: Why are some people not attending regularly?
Will people attend regularly in the future?
Last, Eggplant and Tofu interview five people to find out why some people stop attending the concerts and if more of their fans are likely to drop out in the future.

Here's the feedback they receive:

- "I love you guys! You guys should be a professional band! I am going to brag to everyone that I was at your first show! Of course, I am going to go to every one of your concerts!"
- "Mushroom's husky voice is so soulful! I cried a bit when she sang the ballad. . . . I'll always be there!"
- "I think most of the people were pleasantly surprised with how great you guys are. But, all the songs you guys performed were the same all three times. If you guys keep playing the same songs, the crowd may start getting bored."
- "Eggplant, I loved your guitar solo! I used to think you were just Mushroom's sidekick. . . . what a surprise! There may be days that I can't make it, but I will go as much as possible!"
- "Love the music, but it gets boring when you keep playing the same songs over and over again. . . . You've got to keep the crowd on their toes, keep it fresh. Don't you get bored as well, performing the same songs at every concert?"

It seems like the overall satisfaction level is very high. The two were so happy to get feedback directly from their fans. While it's nice to get praise, sometimes it can be tough to listen to criticism, but both are important when you're trying to figure out how to improve. It appears as though these two are starting to think like professional musicians.

Their key finding in these interviews was the fact that the crowd will get bored and may stop coming if they continue to play the same songs over and over again.

Next, they interview the three people who stopped coming and ask them why they no longer show up. All three answered, "Because you guys keep playing the same songs in the same way, so I got bored." Now it is clear that they need to do something about their show. They need to add some "freshness" to their performances.

By collecting information and conducting analyses, Eggplant and Tofu have disproved their hypothesis and now have a better understanding of the root cause for their lack of concert attendance.

Now they are one step closer to achieving their goal of making Miss Mushroom happy by filling up the gymnasium. They're both looking forward to performing in front of a packed crowd themselves—and one day debuting as a professional rock band.

Develop the Solution

2A. DEVELOP A WIDE VARIETY OF SOLUTIONS TO SOLVE THE PROBLEM

Eggplant and Tofu now have a great understanding of the root causes of their problem. But if they stop here, all their hard work won't have done them any good. Now they have to move on to developing solutions.

Throughout their interviews and analyses, the two realized that they not only need to let people know about the concert; they have to make them want to come as well.

They create a logic tree to help them list the different ways they could get the word out about their show. As you can see, there are many ways to communicate—including newspapers and magazines, message boards, and e-mail—that could be much more effective than just the two of them simply telling people about the show in person. What is important at this stage is that Eggplant and Tofu don't shoot down any ideas early by saying, "Radio? Newspapers? That's impossible!" They list as many ideas as they can and save thinking about their feasibility and impact for later. Even if some ideas sound kind of crazy, they may actually lead to interesting and creative solutions. The key rule here is to list as much as possible and then prioritize later.

Once Eggplant and Tofu write down all the ideas they can think of, they highlight the potentially interesting communication tools on their logic tree and have an intense discussion on how to best use them to effectively bring people to their concerts.

As they go through their options, the two keep in mind their need not just to raise awareness but also to make people want to come to the concerts. For example, when they communicate through the high school radio program, if they announce just the date, time, and location of the concert, all they will do is raise awareness. But if they also air their song on the radio, people will hear what kind of

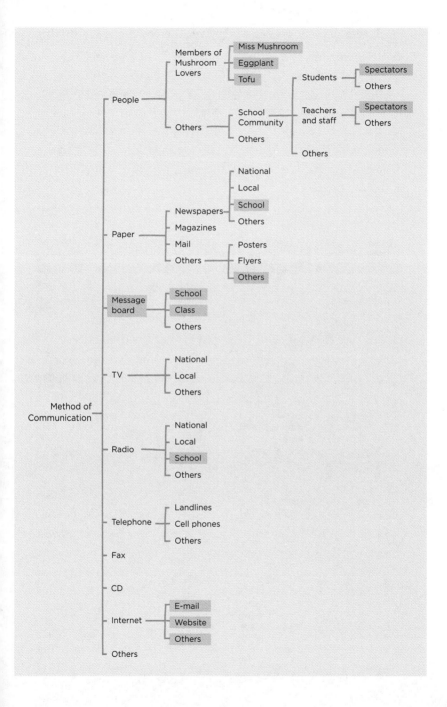

music they play and how great they are, thereby, hopefully, driving up the number of people who'll want to come to the concert.

By staying focused on both these goals, Eggplant and Tofu are making use of the knowledge they gained in the analysis process. If they ignore all that their data tells them, all their work would be for naught. Here's the list of communication routes they decided to look into. They checked off whether each action would (1) make people aware of the show, and (2) make people actually want to attend.

Method	Idea	Makes people aware?	Makes people want to attend?
❶ Members of Mushroom Lovers	Perform in each class during homeroom.	✓	✓
❷ Spectators	Ask concert attendees to invite their friends to the next show.	✓	✓
❸ School paper	Get the high school newspaper to run interviews with the band and fans, and to give the details for their next show.	✓	✓
❹ Posters	Make cool posters and put them up around school.	✓	✓*
❺ Flyers	Hand out flyers to students and teachers as they leave school.	✓	✓*
❻ Message board	Put the concert details up on each class's message board.	✓	

Method	Idea	Makes people aware?	Makes people want to attend?
⑦ School radio	Ask the radio host to play their song and announce the details for the next concert.	✓	✓
⑧ CD	Create a CD to hand out to the students with a note about the next concert.	✓	✓
⑨ E-mail	E-mail all students and teachers the concert details.	✓	
⑩ Website	Create a web-site with song downloads, band member bios, and event listings for their upcoming shows.	✓⋅*	✓

* Dotted checkmarks indicate limited effectiveness.

Eggplant and Tofu added three additional actions to their list based on the findings from their interviews. They decided to change the starting time of the concert and also figured out a way to keep the concert fresh. This is what they came up with:

⑪ Change the concert starting time to 5 p.m.

⑫ Switch 20 percent of the songs to new songs and change the song order to keep the concert fresh.

⑬ Have Tofu tell jokes and stories about the band between songs to entertain the crowd.

Now they have thirteen ideas. But can they implement all of them with less than one month until the next concert? Some of the ideas are time consuming and laborious, and others will require some money to execute.

Eggplant and Tofu are operating with limited time and money. They decide that they'll need to prioritize their ideas to decide which ones they should actually pursue.

2B. PRIORITIZE THE ACTIONS

How should Eggplant and Tofu prioritize their actions? They decide to make their key criteria the potential impact of the action and its ease of implementation, as you can see in the matrix on page 51.

To create the matrix, they rated the impact, from high to low, on the vertical axis. On the horizontal axis, they plotted the ease of implementation, from hard to easy. The best solutions fall in the top right box, with high impact and easy implementation. The least effective solutions fall in the lower left box, with low impact and hard implementation.

1. Perform in each class during homeroom.
2. Ask concert attendees to invite their friends to the next show.
3. Get the high school newspaper to run interviews with the band and fans, and to give the details for their next show.
4. Make cool posters and put them up around school.
5. Hand out flyers to students and teachers as they leave school.
6. Put the concert details up on each class's message board.
7. Ask the radio host to play their song and announce the details for the next concert.
8. Create a CD to hand out to the students with a note about the next concert.
9. E-mail all students and teachers the concert details.
10. Create a website with song downloads, band member bios, and event listings for their upcoming shows.
11. Change the concert starting time to 5 p.m.
12. Switch 20 percent of the songs to new songs and change the song order to keep the concert fresh.
13. Have Tofu tell jokes and stories about the band between songs to entertain the crowd.

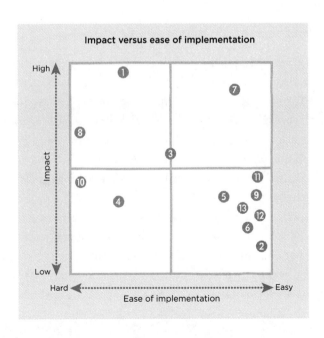

Impact versus ease of implementation

For example, let's see where they should plot number 1 (Perform in each class during homeroom). The impact of this action should be very high: It will not only raise awareness of the concert, but when people hear in person how great the Mushroom Lovers are, they'll want to come to the shows to hear more. However, the ease of implementation is hard because it will take a lot of time to set up and play in each of the twelve classrooms. Therefore, Eggplant and Tofu put it in the top left box of the matrix.

Let's try one more. How about number 6 (Put the concert details up on each class's message board)? Where should they plot this action? The impact is low because very few people look at the message board on any given day, and even if some people were to read the concert details, this will only raise their awareness. Reading the details won't necessarily make people any more inclined to attend the show. However, the ease of implementation is easy because all they have to do is write the details on the message boards. Therefore, Eggplant and Tofu plotted it in the lower right box.

2C. DEVELOP AN IMPLEMENTATION PLAN

So, which actions should Eggplant and Tofu implement? Their first priority should be the actions in the top right box because their impact is high and the ease of implementation is easy. The next priorities are the actions in the top left or bottom right boxes. The least attractive are the ones in the bottom left box.

Eggplant and Tofu have been prioritizing their actions based on the assumption that they would be doing everything on their own. However, what if they seek help from others?

For example, take number 4 (Make cool posters and put them up around school). None of the members of the Mushroom Lovers are good at art, and none has experience creating posters, so they plotted it in the left bottom box (low impact and hard ease of implementation). However, Tofu realized, "What if we ask John Octo-

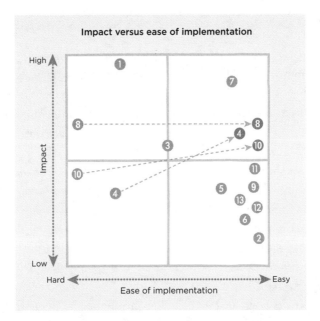

Impact versus ease of implementation

pus to create a poster for us? He would be able to create a really cool one easily!" By asking John to create the poster, the plot for action number 4 moves from the left bottom box to the right top box, as you can see above.

Similarly, they plotted #8 (Create a CD to hand out to the students with a note about the next concert) as high impact but hard ease of implementation because they don't know how to create a CD. However, they know there must be someone in their class who knows how to create one. They can also ask someone to help them out with number 10 (Create a website).

By getting help from others, they were able to pursue all thirteen ideas. People have different strengths. You can accomplish more by collaborating with others who have strengths you may lack.

While Eggplant and Tofu were able to implement all their ideas, that is not always the case. Remember to prioritize your actions and then develop your implementation plan.

THE NEXT MUSHROOM LOVERS' CONCERT

So, what happened at the Mushroom Lovers' next concert?

The month until the next show quickly passed, and Miss Mushroom, Eggplant, and Tofu took the stage once again. When they finished performing their favorite song, "The 3," the gymnasium was silent. It sounded like someone had hit the Mute button on a giant TV remote.

The Mushroom Lovers looked nervously out into the darkened gymnasium. Then the room quickly filled with the sound of clapping and cheering. It was so loud the gymnasium started shaking.

Eggplant and Tofu's efforts paid off! Two hundred people came to watch the concert!

"Mushroom! Mushroom! Tofu! Tofu! Eggplant! Eggplant!" The crowd chanted. They didn't let up.

The three band mates looked bashfully at one another. Their eyes were all filled with tears.

Seeing Eggplant and Tofu crying, Miss Mushroom shouted out, "Hey, you two! Why are you crying!? Don't get so emotional!" Then she suddenly stopped yelling and pulled both of them into a big hug as tears poured down her cheeks.

"Thank you," she said. "Thank you so much, you two."

The Mushroom Lovers' fourth concert was a big success. By raising awareness to 90 percent and getting 50 percent of the people who knew about the show to come, Eggplant and Tofu drew in more than 200 people. And what's more, 90 percent of those people are planning to come again!

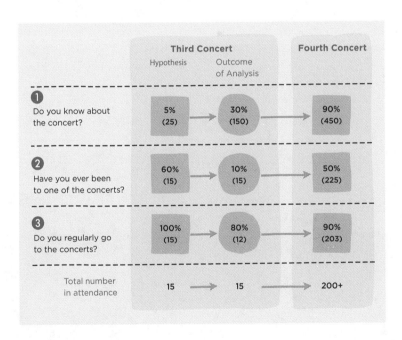

CLASS #3

BREAK DOWN A BIG DREAM
INTO SMALLER GOALS

Problem-solving kids don't just have big dreams; they go after their larger goals by breaking them down into smaller milestones and asking themselves, "What should I do this year, or in the next three months, or today?" These milestones guide problem-solving kids toward their dreams and help to keep them motivated. Once they lay out a plan for achieving a dream, they then figure out the most effective way to achieve each smaller goal and to take the actions needed.

In this class, we're going to see how John Octopus, the Mushroom Lovers' excellent poster designer, tries to achieve his goal. John dreams of going to Hollywood and becoming an animator and a movie director working in computer-generated imagery. For now, his first goal is to buy a computer that will help him learn CGI animation.

There's a proven problem-solving kids' process for figuring out how to achieve such a goal.

- Step 1: Set a clear goal.

- Step 2: Determine the gap between the goal and the current situation.
- Step 3: Form a hypothesis about how to close the gap and achieve the goal.

  3A List as many options and ideas as possible.
  3B Select the best ideas as the hypothesis.

- Step 4: Check the hypothesis. Go back to step 3 if the hypothesis is disproved.

  4A Determine the analyses and information required to test the hypothesis.
  4B Analyze and develop action plan.

Let's see how this process works out for John.

JOHN'S BIG DREAM AND FIRST GOAL

Meet John. John went with his friend Sarah to see a CGI movie the other day, and he loved it. The animation was great, and the characters looked so real he could have sworn they were alive. It was a great story, too. Now he wants to become a Hollywood CGI movie director. He's already imagining the magazine headlines: "Innovative CGI director John Octopus wins the Academy Award," with a photo of him in a tuxedo, holding his Oscar.

But there's one problem. . . .

John has no clue how to create computer-generated animation. In fact, he doesn't even own a computer. So first he needs to figure out how to buy a computer. He'd like to get some design practice by creating his family's holiday card. That means he'll need to get the computer by early December at the latest, which is only six months away.

He knows he needs to come up with a great plan!

STEP 1: SET A CLEAR GOAL

John's first step is to set a clear goal. So what should his goal be? Take a moment and imagine you're John and write down on a piece of paper your idea for John's goal.

What was your answer?

Maybe you simply wrote down, "I want a computer" or "Buy a computer." However, these aren't the best answers. It is important to be more specific.

- Bad examples: "I want a computer"; "Buy a computer."
- Good example: "I want to buy a $500 used Apple computer within six months without borrowing money from others."

The first example is ambiguous. It doesn't clearly state what John wants, when he wants it, or how he wants to obtain it. In the second example, these details are clarified.

- "What do I want?" = "A $500 used Apple computer."
- "When do I want it?" = "Within six months."
- "How do I want to get it?" = "I want to buy it without borrowing money from others."

John has to determine what type of computer would best fit his needs. There are many different types of computers out there. Some are fine for e-mailing and composing documents. Others are better for CGI use, but they can be more expensive. John visited computer shops and searched the Internet, and finally found a computer he likes, a cool-looking $500 used Apple computer. Now he has a specific goal and a number to shoot for.

Next he needs to specify when he wants it. The best way for him to close the gap between his current situation (no computer) and his goal (buy a computer) changes depending on when he actually needs the computer. If he just wants a computer within the next three years, he may be able to buy it by simply saving his money. However, if he wants to buy it within the next six months, he may have to do more than save. He may have to look for new sources of income.

If you have specific conditions for achieving your goal, you should include them in the goal statement. In John's case, he clarified that he wants to buy his computer, not borrow or rent it, and he does not want to borrow money from others to do so.

The more specific the goal is, the more specific the action plan will be. Whenever you set a goal, get into the habit of asking yourself, "What specifically do I want to achieve? When do I want to achieve it? What specific conditions do I have?"

Step 2: Determine the Gap Between the Goal and Current Situation

Once you set a clear goal, you need to identify the gap between your goal and your current situation. If the gap is small, the solution may be very obvious. But if the gap is large, you may have to really think through how to achieve the goal.

Let's look at John's case.

John currently has $150 in savings. His parents give him an allowance of $20 per month, and he earns $3 per hour walking the neighbor's dog once a week, which amounts to $12 per month. But he spends $15 per month, on average.

Will John be able to buy the computer if he maintains his current level of income and spending? To figure this out, he needs to calculate his projected savings in six months at the current rate. If that amount is more than $500, he will be able to buy the computer without making any changes.

Projected savings in six months:

Current savings + number of months x [monthly allowance + (monthly dog-walking income) – average monthly spending] =

$150 + 6 x [$20 + ($3/hour x 1hour/week x 4 weeks/month) – $15] =

$252

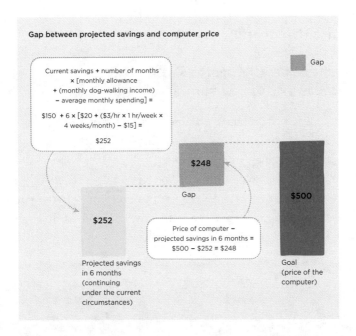

Gap between projected savings and computer price

John figured out that his projected savings would be $252. That means he won't be able to buy the computer if he continues at his current rate of income. He will have to find out a way to fill the gap of $248.

Form a Hypothesis

3A. LIST AS MANY OPTIONS AND IDEAS TO CLOSE THE GAP AS POSSIBLE

John now knows he has to do something extra in order to close the gap. So what should he do? Take a moment to list a few ideas. Be specific as possible.

What did you come up with? Were you able to think of a wide variety of ideas? Sometimes it's hard to break out of your current way of thinking and come up with innovative ideas. It might be tempting to come up with a list like this:

- Ask Mom to increase allowance.
- Save money.
- Buy a lottery ticket.

The first idea probably won't work because John wants to achieve his goal on his own. The second is not specific enough, and the third seems like a long shot. Some people might just give up at this point and decide it will be impossible to save the extra money.

However, by using the logic tree introduced in Class #1, you will be able to come up with a wide variety of more specific ideas. Let's check out the logic tree John has created:

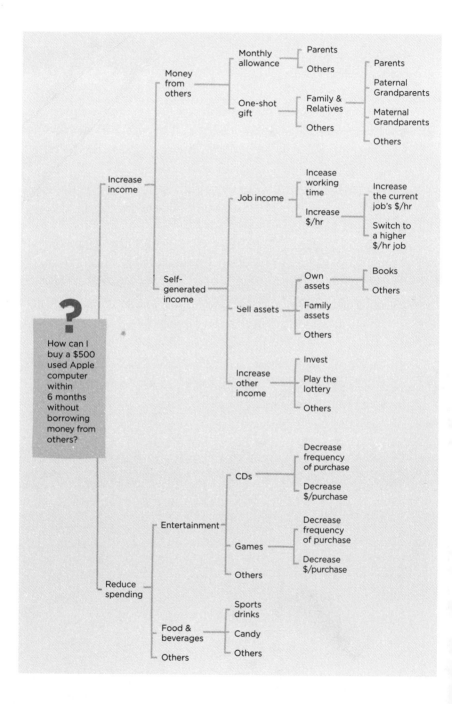

He started at the left with his main problem (How can I buy a $500 used Apple computer in six months without borrowing money from others?). Then he split the first branch into "Increase income" and "Reduce spending."

John thought about how he could increase his income. He created two new branches: "Money from others" and "Self-generated income."

On the "Reduce spending" side, he broke his spending down into the categories of "Entertainment," "Food and beverages," and "Other."

To make the tree grow vertically, repeatedly ask yourself, "Are there other ways of solving the problem?" You can grow the tree horizontally by asking, "Specifically how or what falls into this category?" In this manner, you'll end up developing a wide variety of specific ideas.

3B) SELECT THE BEST IDEAS AS YOUR HYPOTHESIS

Once John created his logic tree, he started to look for the best ideas so he could come up with a hypothesis for how he could close the $248 gap.

You can cut a branch out of your logic tree if the idea is clearly not effective or feasible, or if it goes against your values. For example, in John's case, he cut out the whole "Money from others" branch because his goal is to solve this problem on his own rather than relying on other people for help. He also cut out the branch "Increase working time" because he needs to continue practicing baseball and doing his schoolwork, and he can't afford to spend more time working. He cut out "Invest" and "Play the lottery" because he does not know how to invest, and he has a very low probability of winning the lottery.

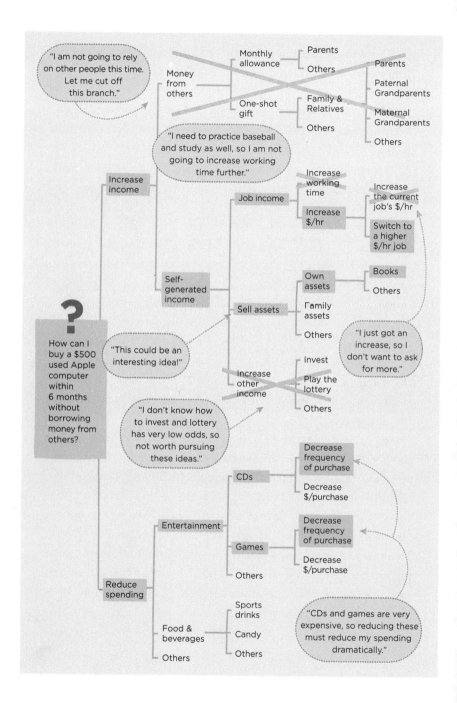

By cutting out branches and highlighting what he sees as the best ideas on the tree, John is able to come up with a hypothesis: "I can buy the computer within six months if I switch to a higher-paying job, sell some used books, and stop purchasing CDs and games."

John used the following hypothesis pyramid to portray this. It shows the main hypothesis (I can buy a $500 used Apple computer within six months), with the specific conditions (the "hows") as the base supporting the main hypothesis.

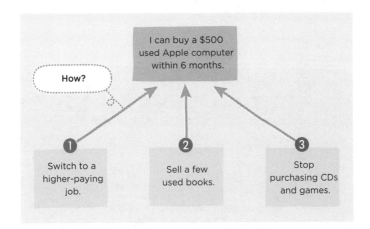

So, why is this still a hypothesis and not John's actual solution? It remains a hypothesis because we still don't know if it is true.

For example, part of John's hypothesis is that he should switch to a higher-paying job. He thinks this might be possible because he heard that one of his friends, Kevin, earns $8 per hour. However, John does not know what job Kevin actually has, whether he has the capability to do the same job, and whether such a job is even available.

But when you set a clear hypothesis and rationale, you are more able to collect information and conduct analyses efficiently, and discover if your hypothesis is true.

PROBLEM-SOLVING TOOL BOX: HYPOTHESIS PYRAMID

The hypothesis pyramid is a great tool for structuring your argument. Using it to clarify your conclusion and rationale before diving into data collection and analysis will improve your productivity dramatically. It's also useful for communicating your hypothesis to others.

The basic structure places the conclusion or main message at the top and lists the supporting rationales on the bottom, like the supporting bricks of a pyramid.

Let's try out a couple of examples and see how it works. Rearrange the boxes in each of the following problems to create a pyramid structure that shows the relationship between them.

Problem 1

School sports are fun.	School is fun.	Lunchtime is fun.	Classes are fun.

Problem 2

Salmon are good swimmers.	Salmon are fish.	Fish are good swimmers.

There are two main types of hypothesis pyramid: the grouping structure and the argument structure. Problem 1 above is an example of the grouping structure. The conclusion "School is fun" is supported by separate but coherent ideas like "School sports are fun," "Lunchtime is fun," and "Classes are fun."

The supporting blocks can be answers to questions like why, how, and what asked about the argument block at the top of the pyramid. For the grouping structure, even if one of the supporting building blocks proves to be wrong, the argument still holds. In this case, you could still make an argument that "School is fun" even if "Classes are fun" proves to be false.

Problem 2 is an example of an argument structure. In this kind of pyramid, multiple statements ("Salmon are fish," "Fish are good swimmers") lead to a conclusion: Salmon are good swimmers. Unlike the grouping structure, with an argument structure, if one of the statements is untrue, the main conclusion is automatically false.

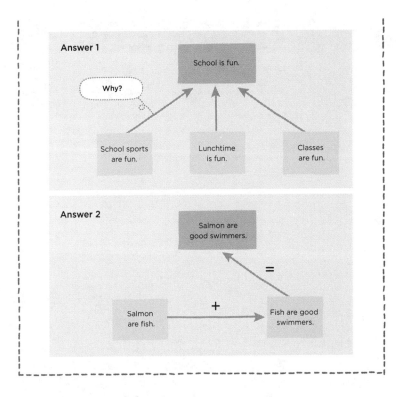

Step 4: Check the hypothesis

4A. DETERMINE THE ANALYSES AND INFORMATION REQUIRED TO TEST THE HYPOTHESIS

Once he comes up with a hypothesis for how he will achieve his goal, John's next step is to figure out what analyses and information will be required to test his hypothesis. As you can see in the following, John used a problem-solving design plan to clarify the issues, his hypotheses and rationale, and the analyses and information required.

Issue	Hypothesis	Rationale	Analysis & Activity	Information Source
❶ How much can I reduce my spending?	I can reduce most of my spending if I stop buying CDs and games.	CDs and games are the most expensive items I buy.	Spending breakdown: Identify my breakdown of spending for the last three months. Spending cut identification: Identify how much my spending can be reduced.	Receipts; my memory of my past three months' spending
❷ How much can I make by selling assets I no longer need?	I can probably make only about $15.	I have only comic books to sell.	Sellable assets search: Look for assets that can be sold. Sell-price research: Figure out how much the assets can be sold for.	My room; my basement Used bookstore pricing; Internet pricing
❸ How much more can I make from a higher-paying job?	I can increase my hourly rate from $3 per hour to $8 per hour.	I don't know what Kevin does, but I heard he makes $8 per hour.	Friend interviews: Interview five friends and find out how much they earn. Neighbor interviews: Interview five neighbors and ask if jobs are available and how much they pay.	Friend interviews Neighbor interviews

In order to test his first hypothesis, "I can reduce most of my spending if I stop buying CDs and games," John decides to analyze his spending over the past three months. He will create a list of his purchases from his receipts, using his memory to fill in any gaps. By separating his purchases into categories, he will get a better idea of what he should cut and how much the impact will be.

He comes up with similar plans of actions for the other two hypotheses, as shown in the design plan above.

Now it is clear what he has to do:

- Spending breakdown and spending cut identification
- Sellable assets search and sell-price research
- Part-time-job-pay interviews with friends
- Part-time-job-availability interviews with neighbors

4B. ANALYZE AND DEVELOP ACTION PLAN

John next moves on to his analyses. First he tries to figure out how much he can reduce his spending.

Analysis #1: How much can John reduce his spending?

He starts by trying to remember and list everything he bought in the past three months: "Okay, last month I bought a $9 video game and a $1 candy bar. What else? Oh, I buy comic books every month for $4, and I buy a sports drink after every baseball game on Saturday."

Using this very rigorous scientific process, John comes up with the following spending data for the past three months:

1 Month Ago	2 Months Ago	3 Months Ago
Sports drink: $1	Sports drink: $1	Sports drink: $1
Sports drink: $1	Sports drink: $1	Sports drink: $1
Sports drink: $1	Sports drink: $1	Sports drink: $1
Sports drink: $1	Sports drink: $1	Sports drink: $1
Comic book: $4	Comic book: $4	Comic book: $4
Candy: $1	Candy: $1	Candy: $1
Video game: $9	CD: $9	
Total: $18	Total: $18	Total: $9

Next he figures out how much he spent on average each month on each type of purchase and creates the following pie chart:

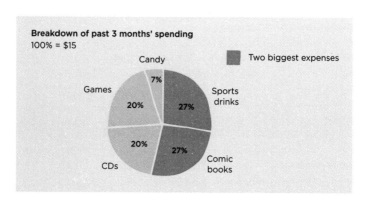

When he looks at the pie chart, John realizes that his hypothesis that he could reduce most of his spending by not purchasing CDs and video games is wrong. He actually spends the most money on sports drinks and comic books. Even though they are less expensive than the CDs and video games, he buys them much more frequently.

John is troubled by his findings. "Do I have to give up sports drinks? And my favorite comic books, too?" he wonders. "I get so thirsty after baseball games, and if I stop reading comic books I will be left out when my friends talk about them at school." It seems there are things John is willing to give up and others that he is not.

Things John could give up:

- Listening to new CDs
- Playing new games

Things John does not want to give up:

- Drinking sports drink after baseball practice

- Reading comic books
- Eating candy

To determine how he will reduce his spending, John has to consider both how much eliminating a purchase will decrease his spending and whether he can give it up until he reaches his goal. Like the Mushroom Lovers in the previous class, John uses a matrix to organize his thoughts:

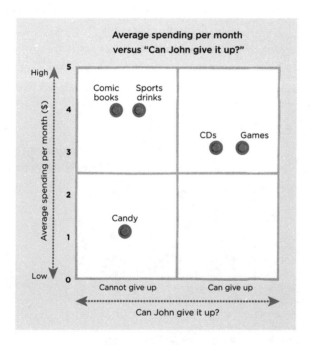

As you can see, he ranks average spending per month on the vertical axis. On the horizontal axis, he places items he cannot give up on the left and items he can give up on the right.

When he plots his purchases on the matrix, it immediately becomes clear that he should give up CDs and video games. They fall in the top right box, meaning they are both easy to give up and have a large impact on his monthly spending. On the other hand, candy falls in the bottom left box, meaning he does not spend a lot on it and does not want to give it up. Since candy doesn't have a large impact on his spending, he decides he need not bother giving it up.

But how about comic books and sports drinks? Although he does not want to give them up, if he can reduce these costs, they will have a large impact on his overall spending. John decides to brainstorm ways he can cut back on these purchases.

He comes up with some brilliant ideas. Instead of buying sports drinks at the baseball diamond, he realizes he can buy a much cheaper powdered sports drink mix, make it at home, and bring it to his baseball games in a water jug. He also decides to copurchase comic books with his friend. He figures out that these changes will cut his sports drink and comic book spending by 50 percent.

Item	What to do	Average spending per month		
		Before	Now	Savings
Sports drinks	Switch to powder, cut spending by 50%	$4	$2	$2
Comic books	Share with friend, cut spending by 50%	$4	$2	$2
CDs	Give up, save 100%	$3	$0	$3
Games	Give up, save 100%	$3	$0	$3
Candy	Continue to buy	$1	$1	$0
Total		$15	$5	$10

John is able to reduce his spending from $15 per month to $5 per month. This will increase his total savings by $60 ($10 × 6 months), leaving a remaining gap of $188 to achieve his goal.

Analysis #2: How much can John make by selling unnecessary assets?
John still has to close the remaining gap of $188. So he searches his room and his basement to find items he and his family no longer need.

He starts with his room. He finds a bunch of comic books and a brand-new dictionary that he has never used. (He prefers to use the dictionary online.) He checks out used-book websites and figures out that he can sell these books for $25.

Next he heads down to the basement. Pushing aside cobwebs, he finds a golf bag his father won at a company event, a baseball glove he used to use when he was in elementary school, and a bunch of old clothes that no longer fit him. "This golf bag could sell for a lot of money!" John thinks. "I'm pretty sure my dad has another one he is already using . . . let me ask Mom if I can sell it. This baseball glove and the old clothes would fit my friend's little brother perfectly! Let me give these to him. I think he would be really happy!"

His mom tells him to go ahead. In fact, she thanks him for

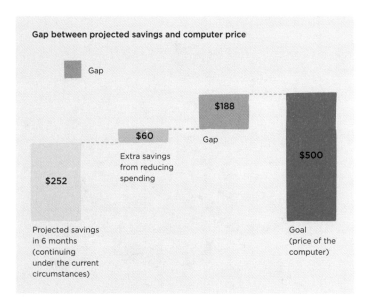

cleaning out the basement. "It's such a mess down there," she tells him. "We have so much stuff we never use!"

John jumps for joy. He runs to the local sporting goods store to see how much money he can get for the golf bag. They offer him $25.

So that's $25 for the books and $25 for the golf bag. "Great!" John says. "Now I've closed the gap by another $50!"

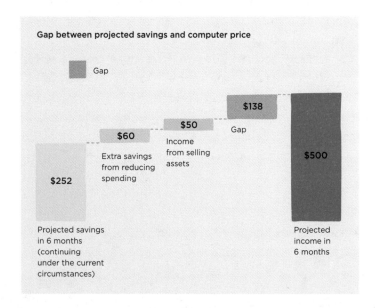

He has $138 to go. Now he needs to find a higher-paying job to close the rest of the gap.

Analysis #3: How much can John increase his income by switching jobs?

John starts out by asking five of his friends about what they do for their part-time jobs and how much they get paid. Here's what he found out:

Friend	Job	Pay
Juan	"I'm a babysitter for families in my neighborhood."	$3/hour
Vipin	"I am bilingual in Japanese and English because I used to live in Japan. I teach Japanese at the community center."	$6/hour
Javier	"I love dogs, but my parents won't let me have one. My aunt lets me walk hers. I told her she didn't have to pay me, but she insists."	$2/hour
Kevin	"I designed a website for my dad's business and word spread. Now I'm developing a few simultaneously."	$8/hour
Pialy	"I walk my neighbor's dog, but he doesn't pay me very much."	$2/hour

Take a minute to consider these responses. What conclusions can we draw?

John realizes that if you have special abilities, like web-design expertise or foreign-language skills, you can make $6 to $8 per hour. The pay seems to be less if you don't have a specialized skill. He also notices that the $3 per hour he makes for dog walking isn't that bad; other dog walkers are only getting paid $2 per hour.

Next he visited his neighbors to find out what kind of jobs may be currently available. Here's what they told him:

Neighbor	Comments
Mr. Wright	"So you need work? You could walk our dog, but we can't pay that much. How about $3 per hour?"
Mr. Kennedy	"Can you babysit our kids? Our last babysitter moved away. We can give you $2 per hour."
Mr. Picasso	"Do you want to do our laundry for $2.50 per hour?"
Mrs. Chanel	"Well, you can walk our dog. But I don't know if you can handle her. She's a big dog, and she barks at people and chases other dogs. But be my guest. I'll pay you $3 per hour."
Mr. King	"You can mow our lawn and rake up the leaves in the fall. How about $3 per hour."

So should John give up, or is there a way for him to close the remaining gap? To make $138 in six months, he'll need to increase his job income by $23 per month, which means increasing his hourly pay by almost $6.

As you can see, John lives in a town with very low wages for students. No one offered him a job that pays more than the $3 per hour he already earns. John is just about ready to throw in the towel, but first he tries to come up with a creative way to increase his income without working more hours. Suddenly, he has an inspired idea.

"What if I walked two more dogs simultaneously? I'll be able to earn $9 per hour by walking three dogs at once! I once saw somebody doing that in New York City! Great!"

John asks the owners of the three dogs if it would be okay for him to walk their dogs all at once. The three are happy for John to do so, especially when they find out it's to help him buy a computer and pursue his Hollywood dream. "You'll have to come back when you're famous and give us autographs," they tell him.

John has come far and now has a great plan!

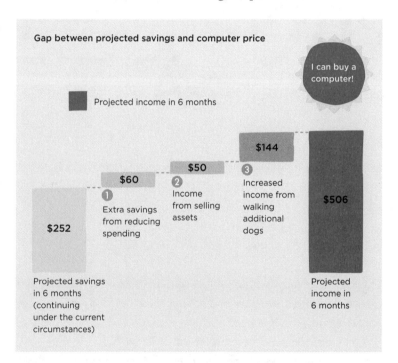

Gap between projected savings and computer price

I can buy a computer!

■ Projected income in 6 months

$252 — Projected savings in 6 months (continuing under the current circumstances)

$60 — ❶ Extra savings from reducing spending

$50 — ❷ Income from selling assets

$144 — ❸ Increased income from walking additional dogs

$506 — Projected income in 6 months

THE MOST CRITICAL STEP: EXECUTION

John worked all the way through the process from the beginning of this Class. He set a clear goal, figured out the gap between his goal and his current situation, formed hypotheses on how he could close that gap, and checked his hypotheses to make sure they would work. Now he has reached the most critical step: execution.

John now has a great plan for achieving his goal of buying a $500 Apple computer within six months, but he can't stop here!

The impact of your actions is determined by the following equation:

Impact = plan effectiveness x quality of execution

To achieve the most impact, you need to have an effective plan and great execution. If you have one but not the other, you won't be able to reach your goal. You need both.

Once you have a concrete plan of action to achieve your goal, don't forget to create a concrete schedule. Write down everything you are going to do, and when you plan to do it.

Remember to monitor your progress and revise your plan as necessary. Very few things in life ever go as perfectly as planned. What if some of the neighbors decide they no longer need you to walk their dogs? If that happens, you no longer have to panic, because now you know how to problem solve. Just use the same approach we've been learning throughout this book!

CLASS #4

SOCCER SCHOOL PROS AND CONS

Problem-solving kids are great decision makers. They rarely regret their choices, because they take the time beforehand to consider all their options and figure out the best decision for them personally.

In this class, we'll see how Kiwi, a young soccer star, goes about choosing a new school. Kiwi is a smart kid, and she always makes sure she knows what she's getting into.

KIWI, THE SOCCER GIRL

Meet Kiwi. Kiwi has loved soccer her whole life. She's been playing ever since she learned how to walk. Every day on the way to school, she dribbles and juggles her soccer ball, rain or shine. She even practices in the snow.

She is short and tiny, even for a soccer player, but due to her lightning speed, great agility, and amazing skills, she grew up to be a great player—in fact, she is now the starting striker for the under-seventeen national team, even though she's still a freshman in high school! Pretty impressive, huh?

Kiwi just got back from a world tour with her team a few days ago, and since then all she can think about is moving to Brazil to train. Her team played an exhibition match against the Brazilian U-17 team—and lost 0–10. There was absolutely nothing she could do about it. The Brazilians were simply better at every aspect of the game. Kiwi started thinking she will need to train and play in a much more competitive environment if she ever wants to be a world-class player.

As her team traveled around the world, playing games in Asia, South America, Europe, and the Middle East, Kiwi also realized that she has a lot to learn about the world. This was her first time away from home, and it turns out her worldview was pretty narrow. Now she wants to live in a different country and become bicultural and bilingual.

KIWI'S SEARCH BEGINS

Kiwi is an adventurous girl. Once she makes up her mind about something, she quickly jumps into action. First she asks her parents if she can transfer to a school in Brazil to play soccer. Touched by Kiwi's commitment and passion, they say okay. However, they make her promise to balance soccer with school work, and tell her she must pick a school where the tuition is less than $3,000 per year.

Kiwi is overjoyed. She runs to her computer and begins researching Brazilian soccer schools on the Internet. She finds the two most famous schools and writes down the pros and cons of each one in the back of her notebook. It turns out that all the starting members of the Brazilian soccer team came from one of these two schools. Kiwi knows she must be on the right track.

She starts with Rio High School, the winner of last year's Brazilian high school soccer championship. Kiwi is impressed with Rio High School's homepage; it's accessible not only in Portuguese, but also in English, Spanish, Italian, French, and Japanese for foreign applicants.

When she opens the homepage, dramatic music plays as a welcome message scrolls across her computer screen:

Kiwi is very impressed with Rio's website. She decides RHS is the school she should be going to. She also learns that the school is in Rio de Janeiro, the big city she has always wanted to visit. "Wow, it's in Rio de Janeiro!" she exclaims. "I can finally try out surfing at the beaches there!" She also looks at the tuition online and discovers that it is just within her budget, $3,000 per year. How could it get better than this!?

Next she looks up Amazon High School, the runner-up in last year's championship. She tries various searches, like "Amazon High School" and "Brazilian soccer, runner-up, high school," but none of them bring her to the school's homepage. Luckily, Kiwi has been studying Portuguese in school. She tries another search, typing in "Amazonas Escola." Near the bottom of the search results, she finds a website for Amazon High School. However, unlike Rio High School, they have a Portuguese-only site.

Using her English-Portuguese dictionary, she scours the Amazon High School website and finally digs out the following information:

- Amazon's soccer team was, in fact, the Brazilian runner-up last year.
- No foreign students currently attend the school, so, of course, no tailored programs exist for foreigners.
- The school is located in the mountains far from Rio—more than two hours away.

- The tuition is $5,000 per year, which is $2,000 over her budget.

Kiwi uses a pros-and-cons grid to compare the two schools. By lining up the benefits and drawbacks of both schools next to each other, she is quickly able to determine which school is a better option.

Rio High School		Amazon High School	
Pros	Cons	Pros	Cons
Great soccer team (last year's national champion)		Great soccer team (last year's national runner-up)	Expensive ($5,000 per year)
Best environment for foreign students (tailored classes for foreign students; many English-speaking students)			Purely Brazilian student body; no programs tailored to foreign students
In Rio			Far from Rio (2+ hours by train)
Cheaper ($3,000 per year)			

Looking at her grid, Kiwi quickly makes her decision: "Amazon High School is not only less attractive, but it is also over my budget. I guess Rio High School is the place for me!" She stays up until 4 a.m. filling out the online application for Rio High School and then goes to bed. Even though it's very late, her eyes remain wide open. She can't stop thinking about the exciting new journey ahead of her.

PROBLEM-SOLVING TOOL BOX:
PROS AND CONS; CRITERIA
AND EVALUATION

There are two tools that are very helpful when you need to evaluate multiple options and select the best one.

Tool 1: Pros and Cons

The first tool is called pros and cons. This tool helps you broaden your options and ensures that you consider both the good aspects (pros) and bad aspects (cons) before making a final decision. Pretend that, like Kiwi, you are trying to pick a new high school to attend. The pros-and-cons tool can help you sort out the differences between your choices.

Step 1: List All the Options

First list all your options; for example, you could have three schools to choose from: Armadillo High School, Beaver High School, and Cougar High School.

Step 2: List the Pros and Cons of Each of the Options

Next list all the pros and cons of each of the options. Even if you think a certain option is the most attractive, get into the habit of asking yourself, "Aren't there negative aspects? Are there other positive aspects?" We tend to be swayed by our first impressions. If we first think something is attractive, we tend to try to collect evidence that supports that idea. On the other hand, if we think something is unattractive, we tend to highlight only its negative points. It is critical to avoid this tendency in order to make a sound decision. Your list of pros and cons for the three high schools might look something like this:

	Pros	Cons
Armadillo High School	High quality of education Strong baseball team Free tuition Some of my friends will probably go there	No study abroad program Far from home Old school building
Beaver High School	High quality of education Study abroad program Strong baseball team Free tuition Many of my friends plan to go there	Far from home Old school building
Cougar High School	Close to home New school building	Low quality of education Mediocre baseball team Expensive tuition ($15,000 per year) None of my friends are going there

Step3: Weight Each of the Positive and Negative Points You Listed

Not all the arguments for or against each choice have the same importance. The next step is to assign a weight to each of the items.

Let's use the following weighting for this example:

+ + +/– – –Very attractive/unattractive
+ +/– –Moderately attractive/unattractive
+/– Marginally attractive/unattractive

Say you think quality of education and cost are very important (so their weight is +/– 3) while the age of the school building is not that important (meaning its weight is +/– 1).

	Pros	Cons
Armadillo High School	+ + + High quality of education + + Strong baseball team + + + Free tuition + + Some of my friends will probably go there	– – – No study abroad program – Far from home – Old school building
	Total: 10 +	**Total: 5 –**
Beaver High School	+ + + High quality of education + + + Study abroad program + + + Strong baseball team + + + Free tuition + + Many of my friends plan to go there	– Far from home – Old school building
	Total: 14 +	**Total: 2 –**
Cougar High School	+ Close to home + New school building	– – – Low quality of education – – Mediocre baseball team – – – Expensive tuition ($15,000 per year) – None of my friends are going there
	Total: 2 +	**Total: 9 –**

Step 4: Select the Most Attractive Option

The final step is to select the best option considering the weighted pros and cons you have listed. In this case, you should probably choose Beaver High School, which has the most plusses and least minuses.

Tool 2: Criteria and Evaluation

The next tool is criteria and evaluation. You can use this tool to clarify which criteria, or qualifications, you should use to evaluate your options, decide the importance of each set of criteria, and effectively evaluate your options.

Step 1: List All the Options

As you did with the pros-and-cons tool, first list all your options. Again, we'll be choosing between Armadillo High School, Beaver High School, and Cougar High School.

Step 2: List the Evaluation Criteria

When you say a school is good or bad, what are your specific criteria? We've been using the following qualifications:

- Quality of education
- Availability of a study abroad program
- Strength of the baseball team
- Estimated number of friends going to the school
- Distance to school
- Newness of the school building
- Cost of tuition

Step 3: Decide the Degree of Importance of Each Criteria

The next step is to decide the degree of importance for each of the criteria you listed in the last step. You can use three levels, like high, medium, and low, or you can use a 10-point scale. We've assigned the following weightings to the criteria:

- Quality of education: High
- Availability of a study abroad program: High
- Strength of the baseball team: Medium
- Estimated number of friends going to the school: Medium
- Distance to school: Low
- Newness of the school building: Low
- Cost of tuition: High

Step 4: Evaluate Each Option Based on the Weighted Criteria

Next you evaluate each option based on the criteria you've set. You can evaluate them with as many levels as you want. For this example, let's use a three-level evaluation method ranging from "+++" for very attractive to "+" for not attractive.

Criteria	Importance	Amadillo HS	Beaver HS	Cougar HS
Attractiveness of school	High	+ +	+ + +	+
Quality of education	High	+ + +	+ + +	+
Study abroad program	High	+ (no)	+ + + (yes)	+ (no)
Strength of baseball team	Medium	+ +	+ +	+
Number of friends attending	Medium	+ +	+ + +	+
Distance to school	Low	+ (25 minutes)	+ (30 minutes)	+ + (5 minutes)
Newness of school building	Low	+	+	+ +
Cost of tuition	High	+ + + (free)	+ + + (free)	+ ($15,000)

As you can see in the "Distance to school" row, you can add specific numbers (e.g., 25 minutes). If you have specific data, include it to be as clear as possible. If something can be evaluated with either a yes or a no (such as the availability of a study abroad program), indicate that as well.

Step 5: Select the Most Attractive Option

Finally, select the most attractive option. Make sure you consider the weight of the evaluation criteria when you make your final judgment. Again, in this example you'd probably choose Beaver High School because Beaver High has high scores on important criteria such as the quality of the education and the availability of a study abroad program, despite low scores on less important criteria, like the distance to the school and the newness of the building.

Both the pros-and-cons tool and the criteria-and-evaluation tool will lead you to the same result and help you to select the best option out of many. But these are more than just tools for organizing your thoughts. They help point out information you might be missing and bring up questions you may need to ask yourself along the way about what you really think is important. Furthermore, you may be able to come up with ways to reduce some of the shortcomings of your options.

THE COMMENTATOR'S GRIPPING ANALYSIS

The next day, Kiwi watched the evening sports news on ESPN, which is a daily ritual for her. There was a special on titled "Why the Yankees Can't Win," and something one of the commentators said grabbed Kiwi's attention:

> "Why can't the Yankees win despite all their superstar players? Put yourself in the shoes of a player who never becomes a starter because the owner (who by the way knows nothing about base-ball) decides to hire ready-made superstars from other teams. The rookies have it the worst. Think about it: These guys almost never have a chance at becoming starters. How can they develop their talent if they don't get to play? A strong team doesn't always equal a great growth environment. It's no wonder the team's morale is so low."

A STRONG TEAM DOESN'T ALWAYS EQUAL A GREAT GROWTH ENVIRONMENT

Staring at the TV screen, Kiwi muttered to herself, "A strong team doesn't always equal a great growth environment. . . ." The commentator had a point. Kiwi suddenly found herself wondering whether she had been using the right criteria to evaluate her school options.

Kiwi reconsidered her original goals: "My main goal is not to play for the best soccer team. I want to become the best player I can by putting myself in the best soccer environment. My second goal is to become bilingual and bicultural."

She jotted down the list of her criteria for picking a school and the importance of each on a piece of paper. As she went through this process, numerous questions started to pop into her head. She started to challenge the thinking process that led her to conclude that Rio High School was not only better but also the only financially feasible option. She started to question herself and challenge her own assumptions.

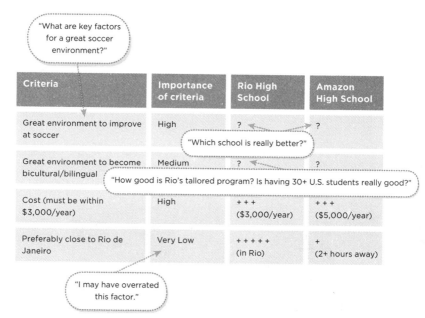

Criteria	Importance of criteria	Rio High School	Amazon High School
Great environment to improve at soccer	High	?	?
Great environment to become bicultural/bilingual	Medium	?	?
Cost (must be within $3,000/year)	High	+ + + ($3,000/year)	+ + + ($5,000/year)
Preferably close to Rio de Janeiro	Very Low	+ + + + + (in Rio)	+ (2+ hours away)

"What are key factors for a great soccer environment?"

"Which school is really better?"

"How good is Rio's tailored program? Is having 30+ U.S. students really good?"

"I may have overrated this factor."

- Great environment to improve at soccer: "What specifically are the key factors of a 'great soccer environment' for me?"
- Great environment to become bicultural and bilingual: "Rio's tailored program for foreigners sounds nice, but how good is it really? Is it really a benefit to have more than thirty U.S. stu-

dents in the school when I am going all the way over to Brazil to experience a different culture and to learn a new language?"

- Cost: "I can't change the two schools' tuitions, but is there a scholarship I could get?"
- Close to Rio: "This is not an important criterion considering my main goals. I may have overrated this factor."

Kiwi made a very common mistake. We often make important decisions without taking enough time to think through the options and to track down accurate information.

As Kiwi started to do here, it is valuable to challenge your own thinking. For the second night in a row, Kiwi lay awake until dawn. But she felt as though she wasn't getting anywhere. Her mind just kept looping back around over the same questions.

"Just worrying and thinking about these questions won't get me anywhere," Kiwi told herself. "I need to figure out what actions I can take to make a better decision." As she jotted down the following to-do list, she finally felt relieved and promptly fell asleep. She dreamed that she was leaving for Brazil, boarding her plane at the airport and feeling full of hope. The dream was amazingly real. She could clearly hear her family and friends as they wished her good luck and felt their arms when they hugged her good-bye.

Questions	Actions to take
1 Great environment for improving at soccer What are the key factors for a great soccer environment for me personally?	• Ask Coach Jones (head coach of the U.S. U-17 national team) what he sees as the key factors for a "great soccer environment."
2 Great environment to become bicultural and bilingual Rio's tailored program for foreigners sounds nice, but is it really that good? Is it actually a benefit to have more than 30 U.S. students at my school when I'm moving to Brazil to experience a new culture and to learn a new language?	• E-mail Rio High School's admission office and ask to talk to a few of Rio's current foreign students.
3 Tuition I can't change the two schools' tuitions . . . but could I find a scholarship?	• Contact the Rio and Amazon admissions offices and see if scholarships are available. • Search for scholarships offered by the government, foundations, or U.S. Soccer Federation.

Finding a Great Soccer Environment

The next morning, Kiwi called Coach Jones and asked him for his advice. He told her, "The most important thing for you is to be surrounded by great players that you get to both play with and compete against on a daily basis." He also told her to get as much playing time as possible. At her age, she'll develop the most technically and physically, and especially mentally, by playing real games under pressure.

He offered some other tips that Kiwi hadn't thought of. He told

her that some teams tend to bench their second- and third-string players, so she should look for a team that offers opportunities for all the strings to play. He thinks the quality of the coaching is also important, although the competitive environment and playing time come first.

Kiwi asked Coach Jones which school he thought she should go to. Coach Jones told her that while he knows that both schools are among the best in the world for soccer, he doesn't know enough to make a fair judgment. Instead, he promised to put Kiwi in touch with Coach Zico, a Brazilian coach who has worked with both schools in the past.

Kiwi thanked Coach Jones profusely for his advice. She was amazed at how simply taking this one extra step led to such valuable information and opportunities. She now had specific criteria to use in evaluating a good soccer environment at Rio and Amazon, and who better to ask for advice than the venerable Brazilian coach Zico?

Later that evening, as Kiwi was walking home from soccer practice, she received a call from Coach Zico. "Hey, is this Kiwi?" Coach Zico asked. "I heard from Coach Jones that you are thinking

Criteria	Importance of criteria	Rio High School	Amazon High School
Great environment to improve at soccer	High	?	?

Criteria		Importance of criteria	Rio High School	Amazon High School
Great environment to improve at soccer	Quality of teammates	High	?	?
	Opportunity to play many games	High	?	?
	Quality of coaching	Medium	?	?
		High	?	?

about going to Rio or Amazon High School. Let me know how I can help." He spoke to Kiwi for over an hour. In the end, he told her that he fully agreed with Coach Jones's criteria for a great soccer environment.

"I would definitely recommend that you go to Amazon," he told her. While he thinks both schools have excellent players, it turns out they actually offer very different environments. "Rio is famous for letting only their starting lineup play games. If you're not on the first string, you won't get much game time. On the other hand, Amazon lets all their players play in an equal number of games. This will make a huge difference for your growth as a player."

Coach Zico also thinks Amazon offers much better coaching. Rio is known for its celebrity coaches, but they are also coaches for the adult national team and spend little time at the school. By contrast, Amazon's coaches spend a lot of face time with their players. "These guys are not famous, but that does not mean that they are not great," Coach Zico said. "I have met a lot of coaches in my life, but these guys are some of the best coaches I have encountered."

Kiwi found Coach Zico very convincing. She was so glad she got a chance to speak with him. She was now able to accurately complete the "great soccer environment" portion of her criteria-and-evaluation chart.

Hi zico!

Criteria		Importance of criteria	Rio High School	Amazon High School
Great environment to improve at soccer	Quality of teammates	High	+ + + + + Great, champion team	+ + + + + Great, runner-up team
	Opportunity to play many games	High	+ + (Only the first-string players get to play)	+ + + + + (All sides get to play)
	Quality of coaching	Medium	+ + ("Celebrity coaches" but not much face time)	+ + + + + (Great coaches; a lot of face time)
		High	+ + +	+ + + + +

103

Finding a Great Environment
to Become Bicultural and Bilingual

Now Kiwi needed to determine how her two choices compared as places to become bicultural and bilingual. She contacted Rio's admission office and received the contact information for three American students who currently attended the school. When she e-mailed the first student, she got this response: "The tailored program for foreign students is well designed. They teach all the classes at a slower pace so all of us can follow even if our Portuguese isn't that great. But if your key goal is to become bicultural and bilingual, I would recommend you go to Amazon. The admissions office may not like what I'm telling you, but I have to be honest. You should really be in a total-immersion environment."

The second Rio student she contacted complained about the number of Americans at the school: "Rio has thirty-plus American students who all take classes together and hang out together after school and don't mingle with local students. Sometimes it feels like I'm still living in the U.S. Many of us still can't speak Portuguese fluently even though we've been here for over two years."

The third student felt the same way: "I don't have any real local friends. If you really want to experience the culture here and learn the language, you should go to a school that only has local students. That's how you'll learn."

Kiwi was shocked by what she read, but all the students had pretty much told her the same thing. The next day, she asked a few foreign exchange students at her own school what kind of environment is best for studying abroad. Like the Rio students Kiwi contacted, they all stressed the importance of putting yourself in a total-immersion environment.

With this information, Kiwi filled in the rest of her criteria-and-evaluation chart:

Criteria		Importance of criteria	Rio High School	Amazon High School
Great environment to improve at soccer	Quality of teammates	High	+ + + + + Great, champion team	+ + + + + Great, runner-up team
	Opportunity to play many games	High	+ + (Only the first-string players get to play)	+ + + + + (All sides get to play)
	Quality of coaching	Medium	+ + ("Celebrity coaches" but not much face time)	+ + + + + (Great coaches; a lot of face time)
		High	+ + +	+ + + + +
Great environment to become bicultural/bilingual	Total emersion (Number of English-students)	High	+ + (30+ U.S. students)	+ + + + + (All Brazilian students; no foreign students)
	Tailored program for foreign students	Low	+ + + + + (Available, good program)	+ (Not available)
		High	+	+ + + +
Cost (must be within $3,000/year)		High	+ + + ($3,000/year—within budget)	+ ($5,000/year—over budget)
Preferably close to Rio de Janeiro		Very Low	+ + + + + (Big city, surfing)	+ + + + + (Small city, mountains)

"Is there a scholarship that I can get?"

Now this was getting complicated. Kiwi now realized that Amazon High School was more attractive than Rio, both as a soccer environment and as a cultural and foreign-language experience, but there was still the issue of the tuition. She somehow had to find funding if she really wanted to go to Amazon High School.

Finding Tuition Funding

Kiwi tried to find an organization that would provide a scholarship for her to go to Amazon High. However, she failed miserably. Amazon did not offer any aid for foreign students. She found some government and foundation scholarships, but the deadline for applying had already passed, and the U.S. Soccer Federation didn't have any scholarships for high school students.

Kiwi is the last person to get depressed, but she had been uncommonly down for the last few days. After all this effort, she may have to go to Rio after all. How painful when she now knows that Amazon would be so much better.

During practice on Saturday morning, Coach Jones pulled Kiwi aside for a chat. "Hey, Kiwi," he said. "How did your conversation with Coach Zico go?"

Kiwi replied, "Coach Jones, thanks a lot for putting me in touch with him. He gave me great advice. I am now convinced Amazon High School is the best for me. But," she said, hanging her head, "there is one issue . . ."

Coach Jones looked concerned. "What is it?"

"Well, I can't afford the tuition. It costs five thousand dollars per year, and that is way over my budget. And I didn't have any luck with scholarships."

Coach Jones frowned at Kiwi for a minute, then snapped his fingers. "Give me one second, Kiwi," he said, then called someone on his cell phone. "Hey, Phil, it's me. How's it going? Listen, you remember Kiwi, right? The freshman striker you saw the other day?

Yeah, the one you were asking me all those questions about." Coach Jones seemed to be talking to someone who watched Kiwi's last game. Kiwi waited quietly, wondering where this was going.

"Yes. . . . Right. . . . Amazon High School in Brazil. Yeah, she wants to go right away. Five thousand dollars per year. Great, I'll have her call you. Thanks, Phil. Let's grab lunch sometime soon."

Coach Jones disconnected the call and turned to Kiwi with a big smile. "Pack your bags, Kiwi!" he exclaimed. "You're going to Amazon."

Kiwi didn't know what to say. She wasn't exactly sure what had happened. "Listen," Coach Jones said. "That was the chief marketing officer at Nike. They want to sponsor you. They're going to pay for everything—your tuition and your living expenses. They'll even provide your gear—whatever you need. Not bad, huh? Talk to your parents about it and go meet him at his office."

Kiwi couldn't believe it. For a minute she stood completely still, but then what her coach just said sank in and she jumped for joy. "Wow! That is amazing! Thanks so much, Coach Jones!"

AT THE AIRPORT

A month later, Kiwi was standing in the terminal at JFK Airport on her way to Brazil. She accepted the offer from Nike to pay for her school expenses. As she said her good-byes to her parents, her twin brothers, Coach Jones, and her teammates who came to send her off, and turned to walk through the gate, her eyes flew open wide. "I've seen this before, this exact scene." She realized this was the dream she had had the night she wrote her to-do list and decided to ask Coach Jones for advice. The only difference was that she was heading off to Amazon High School, instead of Rio.

Kiwi thought to herself, "I guess you can change your destiny if you try to shape it yourself." She smiled and walked onto the plane full of great hopes.

Maybe we'll see her at the World Cup one day. Keep your heads up.

Proactively Shape Your Life
by Challenging Your Decisions

Sounds like Kiwi has an exciting life ahead of her, doesn't it? You may think she was just lucky, but this all happened because she challenged her own preconceptions, because she proactively took action, and because she not only had a talent for soccer but practiced hard over the years to develop her skills. It didn't hurt that her charming and kind personality inspired the people around her to go out of their way to help her out. As Seneca said, "Luck is what happens when preparation meets opportunity." We can learn several lessons from Kiwi:

- Spend less time worrying about things and more time thinking about actions you can take to get closer to your goals, then actually take action.
- Ask for advice. You don't have to figure everything out on your own. Look for information to help you make the best decision in the given time.
- Challenge your own thinking processes and your conclusions. Ask the following questions:
  - What are the pros and cons? Do I have the full list? Which option looks more attractive considering both the pros and the cons? Are the pros and cons really pros and cons? What actions could I take to enhance the pros and to minimize or eliminate the cons?
  - What are the specific criteria I should be using? Do I have the right ones? Am I weighting each criterion the right way?
  - Is my evaluation correct? What information am I basing my evaluation on? Is it accurate, up-to-date, and unbiased? What actions could I take to improve the attractiveness of my options?

We've learned a lot from Kiwi, but even she could have gone further in evaluating her options. Amazon High School is great, but was it really the best choice? She could have looked at other schools in Brazil, or in other countries that also have amazing soccer programs. Of course, she could take only so much time to make her decision, and we all face deadlines. But it's important to always challenge our thinking and to look for other options we may have overlooked.

I hope Kiwi's story has given you some hints to help you make better decisions and improve your life.

Problem solving is easy when you know how to set a clear goal, figure out how to reach it, and follow through while reviewing your progress and making changes to your plan as necessary.

If you make problem solving a habit, you'll be able to make the most of your talents and take control of your life. You can solve not only your own problems, but the problems of your school, your business, and your community—and maybe even the world.

ACKNOWLEDGMENTS

I would like to thank my family, friends, mentors, classmates, teachers, colleagues at McKinsey from all over the globe, the publishing staff of the original Japanese book and of the English edition in the U.S., the illustrators, my agent, and the Delta Studio staff for all the support you have provided, for everything you have taught me, and for making this journey so precious and exciting. I would like to visit each one of you to thank you personally in the upcoming months.

I would like to also send my special thanks to the former office manager at McKinsey, Tokyo, Masao Hirano, my editor Courtney Young, the illustrator Allan Sanders, and the Delta Studio staff, Seita Yui and Takashi Yamashita. Masao was very supportive of my educational initiatives and provided me with the opportunity to write this book. Courtney has put so much time and effort to edit this book—this book could have not been published without your generous and warm support. Allan, thank you for the wonderful drawings you have drawn—they have really brought charm to the book. Seita and Takashi, thank you for the great support for Delta Studio; you have made this journey so fun, heart-warming and exciting.